WHAT'S THA UP TO NEXT?

DEDICATION

I dedicate this book to:

My wonderful wife Christine,
My daughter Sally
My son Richard and his wife Amanda,
My son Paul and his wife Rachel.
My incredible grandchildren:
Ruby, Hattie, Polly, Ivor, Max, Layla
and last but by no means least – Harry
who is here because of the incredible care given to him
at Alder Hey hospital in Liverpool after undergoing
major surgery when he was less than a day old and is now, one
year old and as strong as an ox.

I thank you all.

WHAT'S THA UP TO NEXT?

More Memories of a Yorkshire Bobby

Martyn Johnson

PEN & SWORD
TRUE CRIME

First published in Great Britain in 2018 by
Pen & Sword True Crime
an imprint of
Pen & Sword Books Ltd
47 Church Street
Barnsley
South Yorkshire
S70 2AS

ISBN 978 1 52674 094 6

Typeset in Ehrhardt by
Mac Style
Printed and bound in the UK by CPI Group (UK) Ltd,
Croydon, CR0 4YY

Pen & Sword Books Ltd incorporates the imprints of Pen &
Sword Archaeology, Atlas, Aviation, Battleground, Discovery,
Family History, History, Maritime, Military, Naval, Politics,
Railways, Select, Transport, True Crime, and Fiction,
Frontline Books, Leo Cooper, Praetorian Press, Seaforth
Publishing and Wharncliffe.

For a complete list of Pen & Sword titles please contact
PEN & SWORD BOOKS LIMITED
47 Church Street, Barnsley, South Yorkshire, S70 2AS,
England
E-mail: enquiries@pen-and-sword.co.uk
Website: www.pen-and-sword.co.uk

Contents

Foreword

by Brian Elliott
B.Ed (Hons), M.Phil

Ihave known Martyn Johnson a long time. We first made contact in the 1990s when he phoned me after I was 'guesting' on BBC Radio Sheffield's *Tony Capstick Show*, contributing to the very popular local history part of the programme. Afterwards we became great friends, often meeting at his home in the historic estate village of Wentworth, his wonderful wife Christine always making me most welcome; and occasionally we met for a pint at the Mason's Arms. Perched on a bar stool, his stories and banter were as infectious as they were fascinating; and he was the only person that I ever knew who could 'see' people entering the pub when faced with his back to them. His old police skills and intuitive observations never left him. It was also always a tremendous privilege to meet Martyn's mother Esther, a lovely lady, always kind and hospitable, with a nice sense of humour as well as a fascinating collection of memories and mementoes.

Some of the best experiences that I had with Martyn were when he took me on one of his impromptu 'excursions' to places of interest in and around the locality. I never really knew where we were going but it was always interesting due to his comments and observations. Throughout the journey, he really did demonstrate a detailed knowledge and love of the countryside and an abiding passion for Yorkshire history. Martyn's local knowledge proved to be invaluable during

Catherine Bailey's research for her bestselling book *Black Diamonds*.

Throughout my early association with Martyn it was clear that he not only had a good memory but also a rich mental archive of his experiences as a 'bobby on the beat'. Some of his stories were very sad, others verged on the unbelievable and shocking, but many of his anecdotes were extremely funny. Along with other friends and family I tried to encourage him to write them down as they could be of wider interest in published form.

Eventually Martyn started the writing process, scribbling away at his kitchen table, occasional fags and pots of tea as essential as pen and paper. His unofficial secretary Christine had the job of typing up draft after draft. The first batches read very well and an assembly of enough material emerged 'to make a book'. I was amazed. Several of the early chapter headings were typical of many others that emerged in later books : 'The Hair of the Dog', 'Sergeant Turd and the Mystery Man', 'What a Load of Tripe' and 'What an Embarrassment'. Martyn wrote the way he might speak to friends, which was the best way to present the stories, though I did have to water down the odd word or phrase!

As I was then one of the commissioning editors at Pen & Sword Books I had no hesitation in putting together a proposal for publication at several editorial meetings but was unable to get a definite 'yes', despite my conviction and enthusiasm. At the time I was involved in commissioning and editing many 'true crime' and 'criminal history' titles but the editorial board were wary of taking on a 'risky book' that was of an autobiographical nature. However, after a personal appeal, the Chief Executive gave me the green light to proceed providing that I would work with Martyn on the project, and oversee it through production.

The 'working with Martyn' element included putting together suitable illustrations so that a striking jacket for the book could be made by the designer, alongside a 'blurb' about the content that might attract interest of potential readers.

Many photographs were taken as part of this part of the job but I also thought it would be useful to include some images, for 'plates' within the book itself. The resultant expedition into parts of 'lost Sheffield' that I had never really seen was both enjoyable and worthwhile, even though so much had changed in the intervening years since Martyn's 'beat years'.

What's Tha Up To? sold very well, Martyn doing a tremendous job in promotion in a variety of places and contexts. If only all my authors had the same commitment and enthusiasm! I remember on one occasion Martyn 'sold' the book when sitting on a bench outside Meadowhall, after chatting to a complete stranger. Another sale came from a chap selling ice cream from a van. Similar encounters could be multiplied many times! In fact it soon became clear that his book was 'a winner', gaining a new readership of people not only from Sheffield and South Yorkshire but from far and wide.

What happened next deserves to be placed in a **Hall of Fame Literary Legends**. The book was bought and read by a representative of a major British and international publishing house. It was so highly regarded that a negotiated arrangement was made with Pen & Sword for a new imprint to appear. Within weeks of its new incarnation sales were so good that the book appeared in the Top Ten of the *Sunday Times'* bestseller list, an astonishing achievement and probably the first 'local book' from South Yorkshire to do so in the modern era.

What makes a good series of books is 'a following'; and Martyn had this 'fan-base' right from the start, a large number of like-minded people who were more than happy to read more of his writings. *What's Tha Up To Next?* is now the fifth in the series, another remarkable milestone.

From the start of the 21st century many 'policeman biographies' have been published but this series takes some beating. Excuse the pun. So well done Martyn and you never know there may be a few more stories up your old blue tunic or under your old police helmet! Keep up the good work if and when you can.

Acknowledgements

If anyone had told me a few years ago that I would write a book, never mind being capable of writing a book, I would have laughed out loud at them. Books are written by clever people, not dumplings like me, and I am genuinely amazed at the huge number of people who have contacted me from all quarters of the globe wanting more. I have never been the brightest light on the Christmas tree and am just an ordinary bloke who loves people and laughter. Now at the age of 75 and with the help of my wonderful wife Christine, I have just finished this, my fifth book, which with health permitting, will be followed by book number six.

Without you, the reader, none of this would be possible and I thank each and every one of you for your wonderful accolades and letters of support – I am truly astonished by it all and you are all important to me in equal measures.

All I ever wanted to be was a bobby on the beat and not many years ago I received an amazing complimentary letter from David Gilbertson QPM, BSc(Econ), MBIM, the retired Deputy Assistant Commissioner of Scotland Yard, who said that he agreed with the observations and sentiments in my first books – wow – I couldn't believe it, thank you, sir, for the compliment that you paid me.

It is compliments like that, coupled with many, many more that have helped me to continue writing. When all is said and done we are talking about history, coupled with sometimes sadness, nostalgia and also laughter.

Some of the people who communicate with me I have never met but we are now friends. I cannot name everyone, but I must mention first Joan Ward of Stocksbridge, Patricia

Mills of Sheffield and Doris Turner from Manchester who are all amazing ladies.

Special thanks must go to my Series Editor, Brian Elliott, and Matt Jones and Lori Jones of Pen & Sword Books for putting up with me; and also to Sue and Keith Foulds (ex-fireman), Paul and Christine Johnson, Janet and Jim Fletcher (my old colleagues in the police force), Gill Dakin and Jeremy Scott, Gilly and Derek Gennard, Paula and Malc and Nigel Peat; Pam Radford and Jenny, Mary and Terry Watson and Muriel Leggit from Canada, Sheila and John McMillan; Sally Glover, John and Todd, Jean and Maureen Paton, Freda O'Neal of the USA, Janet and Don Stain, Pam and Ian Walker, Kath, Tansy and Steve Beasley and not forgetting Billy the farmer in Wales.

Many thanks too to Kezia Purnomo at the Curtin University, Bentley, Australia with whom I did a live telephone interview about peoples' perceptions of how policing has changed over the last forty years; plus my new-found friends Margaret Caley, Barbara Ravenhall and Lillian Green, Carol Collins, Janet and Dave Evans, Kevin and Margaret, Jean and Peter Walker, Janet and Keith Pix, Tom Mckie and Eileen Nicholas, Yvonne Hague, Sadie and Susan Knowles, Pat and Doug Mountain (ex-Sheffield United Player).

Finally my appreciation to Victoria Childs and Tony Garnett (who produced *Kes* the famous film set in Yorkshire and about Yorkshire people – both of them lovers of Turners' pork pies from Jump, near Barnsley.

Space precludes me from mentioning everyone's names but nevertheless you are all important to me – thank you.

CHAPTER 1

What a FART!

Terrified – would definitely be an understatement as to how I felt that Monday morning in 1962 as I got off the train at Harrogate Railway Station holding a suitcase. As I looked around me I could see several other men of varying ages making their way to the exit gate and each was carrying a suitcase and a brown carrier bag (no plastic bags in those days), just the same as me.

The driver of an old dark-blue bus was waiting for us and shouted, 'Have your joining instructions at the ready for me to examine and then get on the bus. Do NOT speak or laugh on the bus.' He paused and continued, 'It isn't a pleasure trip that you're on as I'm sure you'll find out during the next three months,' and he laughed out loud.

No one spoke a word as the driver got to his seat, lit a fag and set off. Nearly everyone smoked in those days, including me, and as people lit up I took a Park Drive out of my packet. I was shaking that much I broke four matches trying to light up.

About 15 minutes later the bus pulled up outside a large pair of metal gates with a sign above them which read 'Pannal Ash Police Training College'. We'd arrived, I thought, with a shudder.

Beyond the gates could be seen a long drive leading to a very imposing hall-like building. To the left of that was a large area of tarmac with several groups of policemen in uniform, marching up and down in formation.

We were met at the gate by a sergeant wearing a flat hat with a shiny peak and you could see your face in his highly polished boots. He looked immaculate. He was also carrying a parade or yard stick under his right arm and he didn't smile, instead he had a face like an angry wasp.

We were in civilian clothing and our uniforms, which had been issued to us by our respective police forces a few days earlier, were in our suit cases and our helmets were in the carrier bags.

'Right gentlemen – form two lines – tallest on the left, shortest on the right,' shouted the sergeant.

There were some big blokes there that day and I found myself in the middle of one of the rows.

'This college is where we separate the men from the boys. Now, with your left foot forward first we will march to the front of the building where the Commandant will address you – your luggage will follow on the bus. By the left, quick mar——' … but before he could finish the last word someone in the row behind me shouted, 'I've not joined the police force to learn how to f—— march, I've just done eight years in the Army doing that – I'm off mate.'

At that point another chap piped up and said the same thing except that he'd been in the Navy. You could have heard a pin drop as they both got on the bus, grabbed their gear and disappeared, much to the amazement of the rest of us, including the sergeant.

We finally set off and, after a few RIGHT FOOTS forward instead of the LEFTS as instructed, we managed to get to the front of the huge building in more of a shuffle than a march.

We were then told to 'stand at ease'. Stand at ease, you must be joking! It was nerve racking to say the least and I was ready for the toilet and by the looks on the faces of the other young lads like me they were the same. I was just 19, as were quite a few other fresh-faced lads and I'd come from the small coal mining village of Darfield near Barnsley, with virtually no experience of the outside world; and this was my first outing, if you can call it that, away from home.

The commandant was like the sergeant, no nice words of welcome, just facts and a stern face. We were to be there for three months, which to me was very daunting. I was already ready for off but daren't move.

At the end of each month we were to have a test on all aspects of the law. We would also be taught to march, to do unarmed combat, understand powers of arrest, by-laws, reportable diseases of cattle – and last but not least, strenuous physical education; but after all that, laughter was not allowed.

He also told us that there were female staff working at the centre and for that reason we would be having Bromide in our tea and there was to be no *fraternisation* with the females. I hadn't a clue what Bromide was and certainly didn't know what fraternisation meant. I liked sugar in my tea and it was only later, when talking to some of the older chaps, that I learnt what Bromide was and why it was given to us. Apparently, it was to stop any sexual urges which would then lead to fraternisation, I was told. This place was more like I imagined a prisoner of war camp to be than a training college.

We were to assemble each morning on the parade square in full uniform with spit and polished, shiny boots (again I didn't know what spit and polish was), when we would be taught how to march.

I desperately wanted to leg it as I found myself in a totally different environment to anything I'd experienced before.

After leaving school at 15 with no qualifications at all I became an apprentice blacksmith. I was a big lad of just over 6 foot and 16½ stone and because of my job, I was as strong as a butcher's dog, in fact there was more fat on a cold chip than there was on me. The local vicar at Darfield had coerced me into joining the Sheffield City Police Force and now here I was, just like many others, like a big girl's blouse, shaking like a leaf and ready for home.

My dad's words were ringing in my ears and he was right when he said: 'Stick it out lad and don't give in.'

So, I grabbed my gear and followed the others upstairs to our designated dormitories – my home for the next three months. Home, you've got to be joking I thought, it looked more like a long prison cell with old iron beds lined up on the back wall. On top of each bed, where the pillows would normally be, were sheets and blankets all neatly folded up in an immaculate pile and, to my cost, I learnt later that each morning before parade the Drill Sergeant would come and inspect the neat little pile to ensure that they were all neat and in order. Failing this, and in my case, on the following morning, the Drill Sergeant duly arrived and on seeing the way that I'd put the pile together promptly used his parade stick to rag the pile of bedding. He did this again and again until I'd got it exactly right. But I wasn't on my own and he did the same to several of the others. Some of the older lads who'd been in the armed forces had seen it all before and got theirs perfect.

What a bloody carry on – but I made sure I'd got it right after that.

On the first morning we were there we went down to breakfast and into a large canteen. I was with a new lad also from Sheffield, but none of us were allowed to speak to each other, which I thought was barmy. From there we went to the parade ground and were positioned in orderly rows.

There were policemen there from quite a few different forces. Leeds City, Sheffield City, Nottingham City and county forces like the West Riding, Nottinghamshire County, along with Derbyshire County were the largest. These were followed by the old small borough forces such as Rotherham, Doncaster, Barnsley, Halifax, Huddersfield, Nottingham and Grimsby Town.

Grimsby Town Force apparently had a good football team and only accepted recruits who excelled in the game. Not for me then, I played a decent game of cricket, but I couldn't be doing with football.

The Drill Sergeant and Commandant having told us to stand to attention were now inspecting us one by one and you could hear them picking spots off some of the men for various reasons. By the time they got to me I was 'bricking' it and wished my trousers were brown and not blue.

Here we go, I thought, my turn as the sergeant turned to look me up and down. As he looked at my boots he stepped back with a look of horror on his face, 'Where have you got those boots from Johnson?' he bellowed.

'They're new and from the Army and Navy Shop, Sergeant. They call them 'TUF' boots.'

'Do you know what boot polish looks like, lad?' he shouted. 'Look at the shine on the other men's boots, tomorrow I want to see some major improvements.' He then continued on his way to the next man. As we all left the parade ground after the inspection I was feeling a right twerp, but I was also angry. Mum and dad had bought me the new boots for when I joined the Force and I'd polished them as best as I could.

Back in the dormitory the mood of us all wasn't good. As I checked the other lads' boots I could see that they were all shinier than mine which were almost matt black.

'Now then young fellow,' I heard someone say with a Welsh accent, 'can I look at your boots please?' and I could see a nice warm smile on his face. 'My name is Ivor and I'm an ex-Coldstream Guard and used to people like that jumped up piece of shit – the sergeant.'

After picking up and examining my boots he explained to me that they were rough working boots and covered all over with small pimples and were not a smooth surface which could be polished. He then walked back down the dormitory and returned with, of all things, a table spoon, a tin of black polish and a small candle.

'We all have to learn by example and help each other – you're only a kid and need some help. That bastard of a bully-boy sergeant will get a shock tomorrow when he sees your boots.'

Over the next three to four hours Ivor managed to transform my dull matt boots. It was amazing. After lighting the candle, he kept heating the broad bit on the top of the handle and then holding the spoon bowl, he applied pressure with the hot handle onto the boots – eventually removing all of the pimples. Having done that part of the job, Ivor covered the boots in a thick layer of shoe polish and held the boot over the lit candle which melted the polish and left a smooth surface. Then with one finger wrapped in a duster he started to rub the surface in small circular motions. Every now and then he would spit on the surface of the shoe itself and then continue in small circles as before. By this time a small crowd of young bobbies had gathered round as, like me, they were amazed at the transformation from dull matt to a shiny black surface that you could see your face in.

I thanked Ivor profusely for his help and the other lads applauded. I couldn't wait to get on parade the following morning. I was up early with the rest of the lads and after breakfast, again in silence, we met on the parade ground and as before we stood to attention awaiting inspection.

Even before he got to me I could see from the sergeant's face that he couldn't wait to get to examine my boots in the hope that once more he could make me look stupid in front of everyone else. I was inwardly chuckling as he looked at my boots and his mouth dropped open.

'Are they new boots Johnson?'

'No Sergeant, they've just been cleaned.'

'How the hell have you managed to get them like that?'

And I couldn't wait to reply.

'A bit of pity, a kind word and help go a long way sergeant,' and I could feel my fist clench up – and had to stop myself from popping him on the chin. At that point both the sergeant and the commandant moved on to the next victim – what a pillock of a bully-boy he was, and I relaxed my fist.

The actions of Ivor helping me – a young 'sprog' – had created a bond between quite a lot of us in our dormitory and we all felt more relaxed because of it. It was nice to hear some laughter in the dormitory for a change.

The workload during the day, was seriously stressful to us all and nonstop. We had to learn off by heart this, that and the other which we would be later questioned on. None of us could keep pace with it, to such a degree that at night time when everyone was in bed, some of the lads could be seen using torches under the bed clothes in order to read their notes and they could be heard muttering the stuff that we had to learn and remember.

By the time it got to Friday tea time we were all mentally and physically exhausted with some of the ex-army, navy or air force lads amongst us saying that the disciplines we had to go through were far more stressful that even they were used to.

Enough was enough and when someone suggested going for a pint I was first in the queue. The nearest pub, The Black Swan, in Pannal Village was about three quarters of a mile away and about a dozen of us had a great night playing bar billiards and crib, before staggering back to the college.

We managed to quietly sneak up the stairs and were ready for bed when one of the older chaps put a table in the middle of the room with a box of matches on top of it. What the hell was going off I thought. What happened next blew my mind and it is something that I have never, ever forgotten. The room was in total darkness and we'd had plenty to drink and the older chap explained to us what was what.

'When anybody is ready to fart, shout up and then run to the table, lay on top of it with your legs in the air. I'll be there with a box of matches, and when you're ready to fart I'll light the match and see if we can light your fart! Just remember we want the soft ones. If you fart too hard, you'll blow the match out!'

As I laid there in bed, I couldn't believe my ears and thought I must be dreaming. All was quiet for ten minutes and then someone shouted, 'I'm ready.' I sat up in bed in time to see a chap run to the table, lie on top in his pyjama bottoms with his legs in the air just like a dead sparrow. The match was lit, and you could hear the man give a loud fart. The match flickered and went out and I still thought that I must be dreaming. This happened a few times as the farts were too powerful and blew out the match. About 15 minutes later and with a fresh box of matches at the ready, a lad from Leeds City shouted, 'ready,' and ran to the table. Again, a match was lit, and the noise of a slow fart could be heard and much to my utter amazement a flame was seen near to where the fart came from. The dormitory was in uproar with laughter and disbelief. I just could not believe it and I couldn't wait to tell my mates back home.

The following night we went again to the pub where they were serving pie and sloppy peas which would obviously help with our nightly endeavours. None of us could wait to get back to the dormitory and then men were queuing up for their turn to light their farts. It was like Blackpool illuminations, the softer the better. The pie, peas and beer had obviously done their job.

We were all in hysterics and then a chap called Clarence shouted that it was his turn and he ran to the table and shouted, 'ready'. Again, a match was lit, and you could see quite plainly a soft burst of flame rising upwards and then there was a yell and he was shouting for some water. It was incredible, the dozy pillock had jumped out of bed with no clothes on and the flame had, unfortunately, ignited his pubic hair, which in turn burned his knackers! The dormitory lights came on and you could see that the poor lad was in serious pain. It was serious stuff, but nobody could stop laughing and an ambulance was sent for. Poor old Clarence ended up in Harrogate hospital for a couple of nights and three days later, when his roasted chestnuts had calmed down, we were told that he'd been back to the college, collected his gear and yet another one had left the course.

It has to rank as, probably, the number one of the funniest things (sorry Clarence) that I have ever seen, and I still laugh about it today fifty-six years later.

We were all then banned from visiting the pub and from going into Harrogate for the next two weeks.

On the second weekend we were allowed to go home on weekend leave and I'd already decided that I wasn't going back, but my dad, Fred, after a bit of a row, made me change my mind and so back to the 'loony bin' I went.

By now the camaraderie between us all was good, and it was this that helped us all, including tough ex-forces lads, to get to the end of the course, which was more than some did. Quite a few had given in and left, including one poor chap who wandered off from college, disappeared and was found nearly three weeks later in Snowdonia and muttering to himself. The poor bloke had lost the plot and we were told that unfortunately he ended up in a mental hospital. If it hadn't been for the kindness and help shown to me by Ivor and some other older men that could easily have been me (thanks Ivor).

As probationary constables we all had to go back a year later for a refresher course which I did. Then at the end of the two-year probationary period we all had to be interviewed by our respective chief constables, something I was not looking forward to as I knew my exam results weren't good. On the appointed day at Castle Green police headquarters in Sheffield I was marched into the Chief Constable's office (Eric Stain). After he looked me up and down he said, 'Johnson, these are probably the worst exam results that I have ever seen. And I've no idea what all this 'lighting a fart' business means'. I had to inwardly chuckle as he looked at me. I apologised knowing that I was going to get sacked. Then he spoke again, 'Good exam results don't necessarily make good policemen and he lifted up half a dozen letters from his desk. 'These, PC Johnson, are letters from members of the public who, over the last two years, have taken the time to write to me with glowing reports on how you've helped them in different ways.' I looked at him in amazement. I've always been a people person and talk and listen to as many people as I can. Then he went on to say, 'They are the worst exam results I have ever seen, but to receive six letters from members of the public about your conduct is unheard of. I'm convinced that you'll make a good copper. Congratulations, you are now a fully-fledged police constable.'

★   ★   ★

As those of you who have already read my first four books* know, I spent my first seven years as a beat bobby in the tough East End of Sheffield and loved it. Then I was told to go into the Criminal Investigation Department (CID).

* *What's Tha Up To?*
  What's Tha Up to Nah?
  What's Tha Up to This Time?
  What's Tha Playing at Nah?

CHAPTER 2

Cold Turkey – with a Twist

Torch, fags, three j's: jeans, jumper, a warm jacket – and I was ready for off. As I left the CID office and headed downstairs to the main office, my colleague John Longbottom shouted me back.

'You dozy pillock, you've left your snap on the desk,' and I could hear him laughing. He was right on both counts, but I was eager to get off.

Back upstairs I grabbed my snap box, the obligatory two bananas and followed John downstairs to the waiting Morris Minor CID car.

I was, as usual, as excited as a dog chasing a bitch on heat, as Detective Inspector Hepworth drove us to the premises concerned. Most of our lads hated doing 'stake outs' but for some daft reason I enjoyed them. Apart from it being a change from normal duties and writing bloody reports, it could be exciting, catching a villain breaking into premises and seeing the look of surprise on his face when you grabbed hold of him.

According to the inspector someone had telephoned him at the station and tipped him off anonymously to say that some premises were going to be burgled and, not being sure of the authenticity of the call, he'd arranged with the owners for us to have access, just in case. It could hardly be classed as good 'information' but, as the gaffer said, 'better safe than sorry,' so we were on our way.

As agreed with the owner, the boss dropped us both off at the rear of the building, so that no one could see us entering the premises. We were let in by him but he looked very worried and nervous at the thoughts of his property being broken into. We tried to reassure him that everything would be okay as we climbed the stairs of the two-storey but small warehouse.

First things first: find toilets while the lights were switched on. Then we found the small tea room which contained a kettle and an ash tray. Just the job I thought, knowing that we were going to be holed up there in the dark for up to twelve hours.

The building itself was almost at the entrance of a road leading to a small industrial estate which was very well lit, and the almost full moon meant that keeping observations of our surroundings outside was much easier. Before the owner left us in total darkness he'd shown us the windowless warehouse, which contained pet foods of all descriptions. The two small offices upstairs had no safe and neither John or I could understand why anyone would want to break in at all – there was nothing obvious worth nicking.

Our eyes soon got used to the lack of light in the building and at 7pm John mashed our first pot of tea – only another eleven hours to go!

At the top of the stairs was a tall but narrow window from where we could see any comings and goings outside, so, pot of tea and an ash tray in hand, I plonked myself there. It was going to be a long night. Every little sound or movement kept us on our toes, but as the night wore on with nothing happening, it started to drag a bit – 'come on, let's have some bloody action,' I thought to myself.

At about 1am I mashed and took John his pot of tea, after which I went back to the upstairs office – I was starving hungry and could have eaten a Skegness donkey. Luckily, I didn't need to and some of my favourite mucky black dripping sandwiches along with a bag of crisps, the ones that had a blue twisted paper full of salt inside, followed by a banana, disappeared in minutes. My legs were aching after just standing for the last six to seven hours and it was great to sit down with a fag and have a short break.

It was a cold December night and the heat from a small electric heater at the side of the desk was lulling me towards sleep. I still had half a mug of tea left from my second brew and twelve minutes left before I took over from John once more, so I folded my arms on the desk with my head resting on top of them.

I woke and jumped up in a panic and wondered what the hell was happening in the darkness and at the same time I knocked the rest of my tea all over the bloody desk – what a carry on! There was a loud ringing noise in my ear and then I realized that it was coming from the black bakelite telephone next to where I'd been resting my head. Without thinking I instinctively picked it up and said, 'Hello'. After a slight pause, I heard a man laugh in a sarcastic sort of way and then the phone went dead – 'how odd', I thought, 'what the hell was that about?' All this had taken place in seconds and after lighting a fag to calm me down a bit I looked at my luminous watch – still eight minutes to go before I took over from John at 2am.

By this time, I was wide awake, even after probably only two minutes kip, so after quickly cleaning up the tea from the desk, I went out to talk to John at the top of the stairs and told him what had happened. It was pretty obvious to us both that we were, more than likely, wasting our time and that someone was playing 'silly buggers' with us for whatever reason. There was nothing in the premises worth nicking and with that and the phone call itself, we weren't convinced that anything would happen, but nevertheless we had to sit it out.

At 2.40am a white Morris Minor Panda car entered the estate and was obviously going to check the properties. I couldn't see which policeman it was in the darkness, but I saw him walk down the path towards where we were and then I heard the noise of the door handle being turned as he checked to make sure that it was secure. After that I saw him 'shaking hands' with other door handles at premises near to us, and some fifteen minutes later the car left the estate.

If anything was going to happen at all, then for my money, at 3.30am it would have already happened. John had earlier seen a fox skulking about and between us both, the fox and the police car were the only signs of life that we'd seen over the last nine-and-a-half hours – what a ball-aching waste of time!

We were being picked up by the owner of the warehouse at 6am and, with nothing happening, it couldn't come soon enough for us both. As we opened the front door with the key that he'd left with us in case of any emergency, we got a shock.

There on the step, in front of the door were two frozen turkeys, of all things, placed separately on two sheets of greaseproof paper. John and I looked at each other in amazement – they hadn't flown there so how had they arrived? Where were they from and why were they there in the first place? They couldn't have been there when I saw and heard the policeman check the door just before 3am and our observation post had been manned by one or the other of us, and sometimes both of us, constantly. 'Charlie' or 'Mr Fox' would have smelt them, even though they were frozen, from a mile away, so whoever had put them on the front step must have done so very recently.

Over the top of the door was a small concrete porch which meant that from upstairs we weren't able to see the door or the door step itself. This meant that someone would have had to crawl around the edge of the building when delivering the turkeys in order not to be seen, but why would they do that and what was the point?

A few minutes later the owner of the premises arrived and, just like John and I, he looked at the two turkeys in amazement and simply said, 'Well I haven't ordered them, I don't understand it.'

Someone playing a practical joke is one thing, but what with the premises having nothing to steal, the weird phone call itself, no break-in and then the turkey incident caused alarm bells to ring between John and me. The only people who knew that we were on the premises in the first place was our boss and the owner of the premises – apart from, of course, the man who had made the phone call in the first place to the police station – which was probably the same man who I had stupidly answered the phone to earlier.

It being fairly near to Christmas and there being two of us, someone had probably left us an early Christmas present but neither John or I were daft enough to touch the turkeys or take them home in case it was some sort of a trap, so we left them with the owner of the premises to deal with them as he thought fit.

The next day John and I met up with our boss again at 3pm and outlined the night's events to him which made him also scratch his head the same as us, we just didn't know what to make of it all. A few minutes later the boss called us into his office and sat us down.

'Get this lads – I've been checking the crime reports that have come in this morning and low and behold, a wholesale butcher arrived at his premises at about 6am this morning to find that one of his outside freezer containers had been forced open and a few frozen turkeys had been stolen. The premises concerned were about three quarters of a mile away from where you were last night. The other funny thing is that the chap's voice who gave me the anonymous tip off a couple of days ago, seemed to be trying to disguise his voice for some reason – what the hell's going off, I wonder? When you answered your phone call and the man laughed, did his voice mean anything to you Martyn?'

'No, sir, it was more like a sarcastic laugh and that's all. Then he just put the phone down.'

The boss agreed that there was nothing further that we could do unless our Finger Print Department turned anything up at the wholesale butchers that had been burgled; so after that John and I went about our normal duties, but we were still scratching our heads at the thought of it all.

'Tormenting and banter, as we all know, are part of Yorkshire humour. The other lads in the office had heard what had happened the night before and gave us no mercy but most of them, being townies, said, 'cluck, cluck' or 'quack, quack' ; they obviously hadn't got a clue what sound a turkey made. Others made comments like, 'why did the turkey cross the road and are you suffering from cold turkey?', etc etc. And our reply to them all was, 'GET STUFFED!' (or words to that effect).

The 'voice', the turkeys and the fact that nothing had happened on the stake-out was still niggling away at me – WHY, WHY, WHY? Somewhere there had to be an answer. After checking the night shift rota from the night before I found out which policeman was covering the area in the Panda car and waited to speak to him when he arrived to start work at 11pm.

Apparently, he had checked the premises where the turkeys had been stolen from at about 5am and both buildings along with the outside freezers were all intact as were the padlocks that secured them.

We had to assume that the turkeys which had been suspiciously left for us had to be the same ones that had been stolen from the wholesale butcher. That being the case, then someone must have broken into the freezer unit after 5am – stolen the turkeys and then travelled nearly a mile to where they were then placed on the step without being seen and before 6am when we left the premises. It also meant that whoever it was knew that we were inside the building as well – very disturbing. I'd already checked the crime report regarding the theft from the wholesale butcher and asked the boss if I could look into the matter, to which he agreed. It wasn't a big job but I was intrigued and wanted to know more.

The pressures of work and a couple of days off, meant that it was over a week before I had the chance to call in at the butchers from where the turkeys had been stolen.

After showing him my warrant card and explaining who I was he welcomed me into the office, put the kettle on and invited me to sit down. In no time at all and luckily for me he presented me with a proper pint pot of tea and not in one of those little cups that you usually get in offices. He lit up a cigarette and passed one to me which suited me down to the ground. An interview with a pint pot of tea and a fag – what could be better?

'How can I help you?'

So, I explained to him what had happened to us several days earlier and he looked at me in amazement.

'Well, that's really weird. Why would somebody do that? The other funny thing is that the bastard that stole them must be off his rocker, he only took four – why didn't he take more?' It doesn't make sense does it?'

'Not to me it doesn't.'

'Hang on a minute, when you told me what had happened, did I hear you right when you said the turkeys were left on separate sheets of greaseproof paper?'

'Yes, I did. Why, is that important?'

'Could be. There's no greaseproof paper in the freezer unit but there is in the warehouse.'

'You've got to be joking. On that particular morning can you remember who opened the premises?'

'I've no problem remembering that, it was me, same as every morning. But the odd thing is that on that morning, when I arrived to open up, there was already a light on in the warehouse, which I was convinced that I'd switched off the night before, but I resigned myself to the fact that I must not have done.'

This is getting more interesting by the minute.

'Has anyone else got a key to the premises?' I asked.

'No. Oh hang on a minute though. One of my best lads has decided to emigrate to Australia where he's got a job as the boss of a frozen meat factory and he dropped the spare keys back yesterday – yes that's right, it was the day before him and his family emigrated.'

'Was there a key for the freezer padlock among them?'

'No, only the office keys – if I hadn't noticed the broken padlock on the floor I wouldn't have checked the number of turkeys in the freezer to know that only four had gone – I'm the only person with both office and freezer keys.'

'Did the lad with the keys come into work that day?'

'Yes, bang on 6am just after me – he only has the keys to the premises because sometimes I have to leave early for various reasons and he locks up for me.'

He must have seen the expression of surprise and disappointment on my face and said to me, 'I know what you're thinking but it'll not be him surely – he's a good lad and his pal is one of the gaffers on your job. I don't know how to say this, but his pal calls in for a bit of meat now and again and nobody here likes him, he's dead shifty.'

Then he told me his name!

I nearly spilt my tea all over another desk again, just like I'd done in the 'stake out'. What the hell was going off? I drove back to the office in a trance-like state.

When I was a young and naive uniformed bobby some years previously, this guy was a detective sergeant and I passed on to him some information that I'd received about two armed robbers who had committed crimes all over the north of England. Because of this information they were both later caught, (Chapter 20, *'What's Tha Up to Nah?'*), and he got the glory for the job. About three years ago, when he was in a higher rank, and before I knew him better, he'd asked me for a full report about the 'people smuggling' job. It was to do with Helen, from the café, and her partner 'Sam' and his brother who was a nasty piece of work. (Chapter 14, *What's Tha Playing at Nah?*).

I wouldn't trust him as far as I could throw him, and my mind was racing with possibilities.

After speaking with the butcher, I was left with more questions than answers.

To us it was only a 'ten-a-penny' job, but it appeared that someone had gone to a lot of trouble to steal four frozen turkeys early in the morning and then, more than likely, deposit two of them outside the premises where John and I were doing a stake out. BUT WHY? That was my main question. I couldn't speak to 'Crocodile Dundee' to ask him as he had already left for Australia, and I was certainly not going to speak to his pal, 'Mr Devious Pillock' for want of a better name. It remained a mystery for quite a long time as we shall see later.

I was dizzy with trying to think as to what to do next and with nothing forthcoming I called in at the Mason's Arms in Thorpe Hesley, near to where I lived. The usual lads were in, and after a few pints, a game of crib and plenty of banter, I went home and slept like a log.

CHAPTER 3

A Knight of the Road

The following day was a cold one, which was only to be expected as it was only a couple of weeks before Christmas. As I drove my battered old Ford Escort and joined the recently opened M1 motorway, which then went from Sheffield to Leeds, it started to snow quite heavily.

On reaching the old Victorian police station on Whitworth Lane in Attercliffe, the white snow contrasted against the black stonework of the building; we were in the middle of all the steelworks and furnaces which were constantly belching smoke out daily. Today, it wasn't so bad, but in the summer months when the windows were open you had to have a sweet or chewing gum in your mouth to avoid it getting clogged up with the smoke.

As any good detective will tell you, get your priorities right. After climbing the stairs to the CID office, the first thing I did was mash my colleagues Rick, John and myself a pint pot of tea apiece. One sugar for me and John and FOUR for Rick. After I joined them in the office both Rick and I lit a fag.

As I related the details of my interview with the butcher the previous day and then mentioned the name of 'Mr Devious Pillock', John blew his top.

'Bloody hell, he's a nasty piece of work. Nobody likes or trusts him, and he doesn't like or trust anyone else. He's a devious bastard alright.'

As this point and with a puzzled look on his face Rick said, 'He'd stab anybody in the back, that one! And he'd even lock up his own mother if he thought he could get promotion.' And then as an afterthought, 'Anyway mate he'll certainly not like you.'

'What makes you say that Rick?'

'Quite simply because you're from BARNSLEY.'

'What the hell has Barnsley got to do with anything?'

'The story goes that a year or two back he was drunk in the Club Ba-Ba in Barnsley. He was trying to chat up a bloke's wife. The man whose wife he'd chatted up waited outside for him, and when Mr Devious Pillock left the club he gave him a good hiding, breaking his nose, his wrist and two ribs. It couldn't have happened to a nicer bloke, the bastard! Now you know why he hates Barnsley folk,' explained Rick.

Just then the phone rang. On picking it up, it was the main office sergeant downstairs and he said, 'Martyn there's a bloke here to see you. He didn't give me his name, but he looks a scruffy chuff. I've put him in the waiting room.'

'OK sergeant, I'll nip down.'

As I entered the waiting room all I saw was the back of the man, who was wearing a battered trilby hat with his long white hair hanging down over an old khaki army greatcoat, and I could also see a pair of mud-covered boots that looked as if they'd seen better days. I hadn't got a clue who it was until he turned around.

It was Fred, the nomadic tramp, who I hadn't seen since just before last Christmas. In the summer months Fred used to spend his life doing odd jobs on farms such as fruit and hop picking but as it got nearer to Christmas he walked all the way back up country, calling in at the police station in Attercliffe to let me know that he was in town. He would spend the winter months illegally sleeping in the old brick works on Makin Road in Darnall where he could keep warm. He lived off the land and the kindness of people who felt sorry for him.

I'd first came across him several years earlier when five or six louts were plaguing him until I stepped in, and after putting two or three down the others scarpered. Fred was a great bloke and I think that we'd adopted each other. His white, chipped enamel billycan was hanging down from a narrow rope tied around his waist and because he was out in all weathers, his cheeks were bright red in contrast to his beard that was snowy white.

Going back upstairs I mashed him a pint pot of tea and put six teaspoons of sugar in it to give him a bit of energy – I also took him down my snap box, he looked as if he was starving and I could get some food later from Sarah's café just around the corner from the nick. My ham and tomato sandwiches, along with a banana and an apple went down in minutes, much to the amazement of the office sergeant. I was really glad to see him and especially so after last Christmas.

Over the last few years I'd played Father Christmas at a special school because no one else would do it as sometimes the kids could be a bit unpredictable. My take on that was that my own kids enjoyed meeting Father Christmas, and so why should these kids be denied such a thrilling experience. I'd been asked to do it and last year I'd coerced Fred into becoming Father Christmas's reindeer shepherd and he absolutely loved it, he'd been so good at it that the headmaster asked if we could both do it the following year, and sent him back to the brick kilns with a load of leftover food from the buffet.

Now he was back having walked all the way back to Sheffield from Kent to arrive in time for the kids' Christmas treat which was in two days' time. What a star, thanks Fred. When I patted him on the back to say thank you a cloud of dust flew into the air and a lump of straw fell out from under his old trilby hat (Chapter 19, *What's Tha Playing at Nah?*).

Fred never wore a watch but bang on 2 o'clock a couple of days later, he arrived to meet me at the police station as arranged. He had obviously had a bath and looked fairly smart in a brown jacket, old white shirt with a crimson cravat tucked into the neck and I could see that he'd tried to clean his muddy boots.

Just as before we walked the short journey to the school and sneaked in by the back door as we didn't want the kids to see us. I didn't know who would be more excited, the kids or Fred. He was as giddy as a kipper and, unusually for him, never shut up talking and humming carols to himself. We got changed in the headmaster's office – I put on a big red tunic with a cushion pushed down the front to make me look the part, fastened with a broad black belt; and shiny black boots and a white false beard completed the look.

As Fred was about to don his outfit of a red jacket and green cap, he suddenly spoke to the headmaster, saying 'I enjoyed it very much last year sir and the food that you gave me was marvelous, so I have brought you and your wife a present each to say thank you.' And then, just like Paul Daniels would have done, he delved inside his jacket and pulled out two dead rabbits, still with their fur on but thankfully already gutted. As Fred approached the headmaster with the rabbits he just stood there with his mouth wide open and his eyes sticking out not knowing what to do. He glanced at me as if in a panic and with a finger and thumb of each hand gingerly held each rabbit by one of its ears and placed them on the floor and at the same time saying, 'Thank you, that's very kind, my wife will be very pleased.' At this point I was in absolute hysterics at the headmaster's predicament and I laughed that much that the cushion fell out of my tunic. That set all three of us laughing and Fred said, 'Don't worry sir, if you can't skin them yourself I'll do it for you before I leave the school.'

It was one of the funniest things I have ever witnessed, and poor old Fred was giving away a special Christmas present – the only thing he had to give.

As before, I carried a small bag of Christmas presents in the sack whilst Fred carried a larger sack of presents and a large carrot. When we were led into the hall, with me ringing the school bell and Fred waving the carrot about, the kids went wild. The first carol to be sung was *Away in a Manger*. I could see tears streaming down Fred's face and I wasn't far behind.

The presents were handed out and I had my beard pulled several times and couldn't stop laughing when the kids pulled Fred's beard, not realizing that it was real; and I could see him jumping up and down every time it was pulled. Next came the buffet meal and everyone, including parents and teachers were laughing and having a wonderful time.

As promised, Fred skinned the rabbits and then we walked back to the nick, without our disguises, and he was singing away to himself and crying at the same time. Both Fred and I had thoroughly enjoyed our visit to see the kids at school. We were as happy as pigs in muck and he was already talking about coming back the following year. Weren't we lucky to be able to make the children's day just as they had made ours.

I drove him back to the warm brick kilns with bags full of left-over food from the buffet and his face was beaming with happiness. I was just about to leave when I turned to him, 'Nah then Fred lad, when did tha last have a pint?' He obviously understood Barnsley English and said, 'Now then, let me think! Maybe a couple of years ago with a farmer in Kent. Someone had left a gate open to one of his fields. His horse got out and I helped him get it back into the field.' Then he lowered his eyes and frowned, 'He made me sit in the pub garden because he said that I smelt,' which made him chuckle.

'Come on Fred, jump in the car and I'll take you to a pub with a difference.' I said, and chuckled too.

'They'll not let me in a pub' he said, looking at me longingly, licking his lips in anticipation.

'They will this time Fred, you're with me.'

We drove through the back streets of Attercliffe and after ten minutes we reached our destination. I pulled the CID car up on the snow-covered cobbled street, right near to the red phone box, the one with a small pane of glass missing. I was chuckling about what Fred's reaction would be when we entered the pub. He went in first still wearing his army greatcoat and I followed. The lads in the snug on seeing me shouted, 'one, two, three CID,' in effeminate voices. Fred's face was a picture, and more so still when a big-busted prostitute showing lots of cleavage, blew me a kiss and shouted, 'Hello sweetheart.'

Rick and John were at the bar already, as I knew they would be, and before I had the chance to explain to them who Fred was, a male prostitute (whose nickname was 'Soft Cock'), shouted, 'I'll buy a pint for the big boy and one for the man in Dad's Army. Cecil the barman passed over the two pints and at the same time stroked Fred's long wavy hair. The atmosphere in the pub was always great and you were guaranteed a laugh no matter when you went in. Fred gave me a nudge and pointed back into the snug saying, 'That blond-haired woman looks a bit of alright.' I turned to see George take off his long blonde wig and put it on the bar. What a sight. For a change Fred had stopped talking and just looked around him in total awe at what he was seeing. Two old black men, who were regulars, were playing dominoes as usual and Big Basil, who hired himself out to rich women, was dancing to the music from the jukebox. It was, without doubt, the most unusual and yet friendly pub that Rick, John and I called in now and again.

Both Rick and John had heard about Fred but had never met him, and they were chuckling as they looked at his state of bewilderment at what he was witnessing. We all raised a glass to Fred and wished him all the very best for Christmas and I thanked him for helping out once more and making the kids' day.

I then asked Fred to tell Rick and John the story about how he had brought two rabbits for the headmaster and they laughed out loud.

'Were they skinned?' John asked Fred.

'No,' said Fred, 'I'd snared and gutted them, but I'd not had time to skin them – looking at the headmaster's face I don't think that he'd seen a rabbit before either dead or alive and they're really good eating.'

Fred was right, from the age of round about twelve, back in my home village, I used to snare rabbits, gut them and skin them and the local poacher used to sell loads of them to hospitals. If someone had had a stomach or intestinal operation that was the first meat that they would serve, as it was so easy for them to both eat and digest; and as for rabbit gravy, you can't beat it, and that's coming from someone who doesn't like any other gravy.

I was also a bit surprised at the headmaster's reaction because, in the early '60s and quite a while after, rabbits, hares, pheasants, partridge, ducks and quail were always hung outside any good butcher's shop. People today don't know what's good for them, unless its frozen; they don't know what they're missing.

Fred's first pint had already gone, and he was quickly onto his second, closely followed by his third and like the girls in the back room he started to dance to the sound coming from the jukebox. He was having a great time. I never drank more than a pint and a half when I was driving, and it was a shame when I had to drag him away. He was singing Christmas carols all the way back to the brick kilns and could hardly stand up when I let him out of the car.

'Thanks for a marvelous day out, Martyn,' he slurred, 'have a good Christmas.' He shook my hand warmly and staggered off.

On odd occasions, over the next few weeks, I looked in on him in the early evening. Tom, the night watchman at the kilns, had given him odd jobs to do which kept him going until the end of March when he would set off on his long walk back down south.

The day before he left I took him a bottle of beer and a freshly made pork pie. He looked as fit as a flea and I bade him goodbye.

I knew that in about nine months' time he'd be back up North to do an encore at the school. I waited and waited but still no Fred and I had to do it on my own which wasn't the same. Everyone else missed him as well, especially the children and I am sad to say that after a couple of years waiting I realized that my good friend Fred, must have passed away. He was a wonderful man and a gentleman and every Christmas since then I spare a thought and raise a glass to him. To Fred, a true Knight of the Road.

CHAPTER 4

HELP! What a Nightmare – Squawk, Squawk

Over the Christmas period I put the turkey fiasco behind me. I couldn't stop thinking about the kids at the special school. Seeing their smiling faces and hearing them and their parents laughing is what, to me, life should be all about – happiness. It also made me realize how much I was missing working the beat. I'd been a detective now for nearly two years and was certainly not enjoying it as much as when I was on the beat. The thing that I was missing the most were the kids at school time, who were always wanting to chat and the old people who were often lonely with no one to talk to. Five minutes banter with them was all it took to make them smile and feel less lonely. Shopkeepers were the same, and if ever I was short of a pot of tea I could nip in here, there and everywhere – which was all part of the public relations which could collectively lead to gathering information about who was doing this, that or the other.

My reason for joining the police force in the first place was to take an active part in helping within the community. I have always loved people and try to work with them as opposed to against them. Some people are born in one country, whilst some are born in another – often thousands of miles apart. Whatever our skin colour, we are all made from the same component parts. Some people are rich, whilst some others can barely survive. Some people are clever and some, like me, were born not so clever, which suits me down to the ground and allows me to live a simple and uncomplicated life.

As a nipper it was drilled into me by my parents to help people who needed it. They then went on to explain to me that the act of helping someone makes them feel good, as well as yourself for having done so. My parents were right, and over many years, I've made plenty of friends through my actions of helping out. It also works the other way around and I've made friends with people when I have sometimes needed help myself. But does it always work out right? I'll give you two examples. Let's see what you think.

As any bobby will tell you, decisions sometimes have to be made in seconds, and without the benefit of hindsight.

Several years before I became a detective, I was riding my old 'sit-up-and-beg' police push bike whilst on the beat on City Road, on the Manor Estate. It was a rough area to work and a place where I'd had several scraps with the local villains in the past.

There were a lot of people on the pavements of the busy main road and I noticed a young woman pushing a pushchair, inside of which was a little toddler of about three years of age. As I got nearer the woman suddenly stopped walking and bent down to look into the pushchair and she was frantically pulling off all the covers from around the baby. She looked most upset. Pulling up beside her I asked her what was wrong, and could I help in any way. She was beside herself with worry and told me that she couldn't find her purse, and promptly started to cry. I tried to calm her down a bit and then asked when she had last seen her purse.

'I needed some change to make a phone call – I wonder if I've left it in the phone box down the road?' and she pointed towards the red telephone kiosk about 200 yards away and continued, 'That was about 10 minutes ago and by the time I get there someone will have already nicked it, you know what they're like round here.'

There were no mobile phones back then and, in a busy area like this one, you sometimes had to queue at the kiosk before you could make a telephone call. I would have to be quick in case someone got there before me and stole the purse. I told the young lady to wait where she was, and I shot off.

Bradley Wiggins or Mark Cavendish wouldn't have had a chance of catching me as I sped down the road on my heavy pushbike. She was lucky that day, the purse was still there, so I grabbed it and sped back to her. I was puffing and panting like an old man, but I was also dead chuffed about my good deed for the day as I passed the purse back to her.

'Thank you, thank you, thank you. My week's housekeeping money is in there.'

Then, standing on her tiptoes she leaned forward and gave me a kiss on the cheek. I felt a right twerp being in full uniform and I also remember blushing. A rough looking bloke shouted, 'Fancy kissing a copper!' and then he too laughed and clapped as did the small crowd that had gathered, presumably having been told of the situation by the young lady when I'd cycled off to find her purse.

As I cycled away I was feeling a bit daft because of the young lady kissing me, but I was also thrilled to bits that we'd sorted out the problem. Just then I heard someone shout the word 'officer', and I turned to see the small crowd beckoning me back. As I approached them I could see that the young woman was sobbing and as I got to her she said, 'there's no money left in my purse, it's been stolen.'

What a bloody idiot I am, I thought. I should have stayed there to witness the purse being opened and I knew that I was now in an awkward situation – I was the last person to handle the now empty purse. Whilst walking with her away from the crowd, it gave me the chance to decide what to do next. Her name was Hattie and I asked her how much she had in the purse.

'I don't know exactly,' she said, sobbing, 'I'm a single mother and I had just collected my weekly allowance from the Benefits Office, because that is the only way I can survive.'

At this stage I was beginning to wonder if this was a set-up, so I quite simply said to her, 'Let's walk up to the police sub-station where I'll take a report,' to which she thankfully agreed, as there was no way that I was letting her out of my sight.

We sat down in the office and I nonchalantly phoned the on-duty inspector, outlining the situation to him and the fact that we were both remaining in the same room. I also told him (which wasn't true) that I'd sprained my wrist and could he come straight away to take a report off her. He replied without the young woman hearing, 'You've done exactly the right thing in ringing me Johnson, do not leave her on her own, I'm on my way and I'll be there in about fifteen minutes.' He'd obviously understood my predicament.

On his arrival at the one-roomed sub-station he introduced himself and took a statement off Hattie and then at that point he asked the girl point blank, 'Have you any complaint about the way that my officer dealt with the problem?'

She looked at him with her mouth open and said, 'None whatsoever. He did a marvelous job by immediately finding and bringing my purse back to me.'

At that point the inspector explained to her that when pick pockets or opportunist thieves steal a purse, handbag or other small items, the first thing they do is to grab the money and dispose of the purse, handbag or whatever it was that they had stolen, so that no item is found on them that can connect them to the crime.

She looked surprised. I then told the inspector that I would like him to search me in the presence of Hattie. Both Hattie and the Inspector said that there was no need, but I still insisted on being searched. People can say or think anything after being in a situation like that and that's why I wanted to be searched there and then. Taking off my jacket, I emptied my pockets, opened my shirt and they both realized that I hadn't got anything hidden on me. After the inspector wrote a crime report Hattie went on her way back to explain to the Benefits Office what had happened in the hope that they could help. Unfortunately, the culprit was never caught, and it reinforced to me, what all coppers will tell you, always expect the unexpected.

★   ★   ★

Another HELP-ME incident occurred just after I had become a detective. One late sunny afternoon I was driving a marked police Panda car instead of one of the plain CID cars as they were tied up on other jobs. I was looking into several burglaries which had taken place in the infamous Parson Cross area of the city after having been given some information from a local shop keeper that I knew. He'd given me the 'nod' and said that it might be 'Mr Housebreaker', who'd already got several convictions for breaking and entering. Rumour had it that he had been kicked out of his rented property and was now living rough somewhere in the Chapeltown area, so I was having a drive round to see if I could 'sniff' him out.

As I drove through the historic village of Ecclesfield, I noticed a group of children, along with a couple of adults and an old lady dressed in a long pinafore over her dress. All were looking upwards and pointing into a large tree at the side of the road.

What's up with them I thought, and, being nosy decided to pull the police car up at the side of them to see what was going off. As I got out nobody noticed me, and they were still looking and pointing up at the tree, all except the old lady who was now crying. As I stood back and looked up into the tree, near to the top I could see, of all things, a parrot. I nearly dropped bow legged and couldn't believe what I was seeing. When I asked some kids in the crowd who the parrot belonged to, they pointed to the old lady, so I went to speak to her.

'He's mine mister. I was cleaning his cage when he flew out of it and straight through the back door which I'd stupidly left open. He did the same thing about two years ago and flew into that same tree but not as high up as he is now, so a young man caught him for me. Please help me mister. He's my companion and the only friend I see or talk to all day. I don't know what I'd do if I lost him.'

As a youngster me and my mate, Roy, were always climbing trees in the summer and mainly in the vicarage orchard where we picked apples and pears galore (with the vicar's permission of course).

The word HELP had cropped up again. I decided to give it a go even though the bird was sat on the end of a branch about 25 to 30ft up in the tree. The tree was inside Ecclesfield churchyard so, with jacket off, I 'skrimmed' up the churchyard wall, and at the same time realized what I was about to do was madness. A local chap had found and passed to me a triangular-shaped fishing landing net which had a long metal handle. Just the thing, I thought. Johnny Weissmuller, or Tarzan, would have been proud of me that day as I slowly made my way up the trunk of the old yew tree.

In fairness, it was easy to climb as the trunk was full of stub ends of old branches that had been pruned as the tree grew. In no time I was up to the long branch where 'Mr Polly Parrot' was looking at me from the end of what was a thin branch. Without the fishing net I wouldn't have stood a chance but as I very slowly and gingerly started to shin along the branch I could also feel it sagging with my weight.

What the bloody hell am I doing up here, I must be mad.

When I glanced down at the crowd I was a lot higher up than I'd anticipated, and Tarzan Johnson wasn't as brave anymore. An inch at a time, I moved further along the sagging branch with my arm outstretched whilst holding the long-handled net, until I was within striking distance. Luckily the parrot was tame and made no attempt to move. As he looked at me he seemed to be more frightened than I was!

Holding onto the branch with my left arm I gently got the net near to Polly and then a split second later I had him. I could hear the crowd down below cheering, even above the parrot's loud squawks. Slowly I retreated down the tree trunk. The fisherman below had been much cleverer than I was and had sensibly attached a clothes line to the loop at the end of the handle, so, after twisting the net round a few times so that the parrot couldn't get out, I was able to slowly lower the bird to the ground, leaving me the next problem of getting down the bloody tree.

Nearly all detectives wear suits, including me, but in the summer months I used to help the gamekeepers in the parkland at Wentworth when they were rearing the young pheasants at the back of the biggest house in Europe, Wentworth Woodhouse and for that I used to wear either moleskin or cord trousers. Today, I was wearing my cord trousers, the material of which was fairly slippy, and now that the parrot had been caught I was about to inch my way down the tree when two things happened.

The bark of the tree was shiny in places and, because of my cord trousers, I slid with my left leg and started to slide down the tree and had nothing to grip on to. I seriously thought that I was a goner but just as I thought this I felt a huge tug on my leather belt which brought me to a sudden halt. To say I was lucky would be an understatement. The stub of an old branch, as I slid down the tree, got between the top of my trousers and under my belt where the buckle was, but I was well and truly stuck. I couldn't grip with my hands or my feet and I was just hung there like a stuffed dummy. I could hear the kids screaming about 20ft below me, but there was nothing that I could do.

If I'd undone my belt, which had saved me from falling, I'd have plummeted into the churchyard, the thoughts of which made me shudder. After what seemed like an eternity of not knowing what to do I heard the sound of a bell coming towards me but didn't know what it was.

I was seriously lucky that day, one of the adults down below, who turned out to be a teacher, had the sense to ring for the fire brigade who had a turntable ladder and after fastening a harness around my chest, the firemen were then able to pull me up off the stub of the branch and get me onto the ladder where I was then lowered down to the ground, much to my absolute embarrassment. The kids were cheering, the old lady was crying, the parrot was squawking and I was walking like John Wayne. I'd been hanging up in the tree with my nuts carrying all my weight because my trouser crotch had been pressing on them for about twenty minutes whilst I was hanging from my belt.

The old lady was over the moon with the return of her parrot and once more I got a kiss on the cheek for my trouble.

A few days later Mr Housebreaker was caught during a house burglary in, of all places, Ripon in North Yorkshire. After his arrest his record was checked. It was discovered that I had circulated his details and the fact that he was wanted by us in Sheffield; and was due to stand trial for about twenty house burglaries.

Later I had to go to court in Harrogate, which is near Ripon. He pleaded guilty to both the Ripon job and our own, and I had the pleasure of seeing him sentenced to two-and-a-half-years in the 'slammer' (prison). Without the HELP of the police at Ripon he might have carried on doing more burglaries, so on that occasion, as with the lost parrot, HELP played its part again.

★   ★   ★

Note:

I am sure that you already help people, but if we all helped more, then the world would be a happier place to live in – remember, being charitable blesses those who give as well as those who receive.

CHAPTER 5

Now You See it – Now You Don't

As a youngster brought up in the small coal mining village of Darfield, near Barnsley, I grew up in the shadow of one of the most beautiful and oldest churches in, what was then, the old West Riding of Yorkshire. All Saints Church stood on a promontory overlooking the confluence of the River Dove and the River Dearne. A few miles down river the Dearne joined the mighty River Don, which like the Dearne, had started life as a trickle in the foothills of the Pennines, high above Penistone. As it gathered more water where other streams joined it, the Don also gathered more power as it passed through Stocksbridge, Deepcar, Sheffield, Rotherham, Mexborough and Doncaster and then, about 70 miles from its source it emptied into the River Humber near Goole in East Yorkshire and from there into the North Sea. All along its length, and because of its power, sprouted up water-driven mills and forges which, from medieval days, were used in the manufacture of different items in the cutlery and allied trades. Anything made of metal, and especially knives which needed a sharp edge, were dependent upon the mills, and, as everyone knows, famous Sheffield cutlery was exported all over the world.

During the Industrial Revolution, businesses in the towns and cities of what is now South Yorkshire, such as those already mentioned, grew at an incredible rate as did the population; and people travelled from all over the country to seek employment in the new industrial north.

Darfield church has been standing on the same spot for well over a thousand years and it was only about a mile away from there that I found a large hoard of Roman coins in a builder's trench when I was seven years old. It is my belief that the Romans used the rivers to transport commodities, such as salt, lead and mill stones back to Rome and bring to England anything that the Roman armies needed.

When my dad, Fred, was a young lad he was the church organ blower, making sure, with the aid of bellows, that there was enough air in the organ valves to enable it to make a tune. When I was about eight years old I was told to join the church choir (don't laugh) and I loved it. Also in the choir was John McMillan and his dad, an ex-naval commander and Sheila Croft, the daughter of my dad's best pal, Jack Croft, another great guy. John went on to marry Sheila and they are still today two of the nicest people you could ever wish to meet; and are our good friends. John's brother, Ian McMillan is the now famous broadcaster, TV and radio star 'The Bard of Barnsley', a brilliantly clever bloke, and to think that I sometimes used to push him around the village in his pushchair when he was small – well done Ian, lad.

When the choir sang at a wedding, we got paid one shilling (5p in today's money). Just up the road from the church was Camplejohn's shop where we could spend our well-earned cash. They were lovely people. Every Christmas the choir would walk around the village carrying an old lantern at the end of a pole and call in at Camplejohns's shop and all the pubs, singing Christmas carols, which to us as nippers, was quite exciting.

When Mr Camplejohn retired, the shop was taken over by two men, Maurice Dobson and Fred Halladay and I was later to be told that they were both gay, which didn't mean a thing to me. Both Maurice and Fred were well-known for their growing collection of antiques of every description, and as I grew older I also became interested in antiques. After joining the police force and getting married to Christine we would often visit the shop after closing time and sometimes take along friends with us. Maurice and Fred loved visitors, especially if they could talk antiques.

One of the attractions to me, apart from the antiques, was a full-sized snooker table that we would often play on. After a game of snooker, we would sit down, have a chat and a glass of sherry. Maurice would always go to his old pipe rack and take an ancient church warden's clay pipe out. It was curved and about 15 inches long, and was part of his collection. He'd fill it with tobacco and took pleasure in seeing me smoke it. Neither of them were smokers and I used to sit there puffing away. They were great people and we always had a good laugh with them. They didn't drive and for that reason we often conveyed them to antique fairs or antique shops within a radius of about fifty miles, and they taught us a lot.

One day, Christine rang me up at work to tell me that Maurice and Fred had got four tickets for the following weekend to visit the annual antique dealers' fair in Harrogate and could we take them. They would pay for the petrol and entrance tickets. Luckily it fell on my weekend off and neither Christine or myself could wait. They knew their stuff whilst we were still learning.

Antique fairs in the early 1970s weren't as common as they are today and were usually reserved for dealers only. If you wished to purchase anything at the fair you had to be in the 'trade' and produce a business card to prove it. That being the case then you could try and haggle to get the price down to what you were prepared to pay.

Fred was the quiet one of the two, and when Christine and I picked them up he was wearing an ordinary pair of trousers and a jumper. Maurice, however, was the theatrical and flamboyant one, just like the business card he'd made – pale pink with a fancy scalloped edge. He was wearing a blue pinstriped suit with a yellow handkerchief sticking out of his breast pocket, along with a pair of cream brogue shoes and a yellow cravat, he looked the part.

Maurice's looks and gender (he sometimes wore red lipstick but luckily for us not that day) were very beguiling. I think he was an ex-soldier in one of the Scottish Highland Regiments, and he stood no nonsense. He was very well-known in the Barnsley and Wombwell areas and my dad used to tell me that many a man who'd tormented him about the way he looked and acted ended up with a broken nose and several teeth missing. He was easy to get along with and I never heard anyone in the village have anything bad to say about him. He was, quite simply, a character. At one point I even thought about taking him to Mucky Mary's to meet George with the long blonde wig, and Doreen (Soft Cock) but I imagined what could go wrong and so decided against it.

On our way we drove through Leeds, passing one of my favourite country houses, Harewood House, and then Pannal Ash Police Training College, where I'd done my training several years earlier. From there we travelled into Harrogate itself.

The place that we were in was huge and as Christine and myself slowly walked round I couldn't believe the age and quality of the pieces on sale. It was all 'top drawer' stuff. There were dealers there from all over the British Isles and one selling specialist glassware from Paris. The prices were incredible, but it didn't seem to put off the many people who were there. Looking across the room I could see Maurice and Fred haggling with a dealer over the price of a fantastic looking Welsh dresser. We left them to it and went for a pot of tea and a scone – all we could afford at those prices – after which I went to use the toilet. As I was leaving the gents I saw a youngish man with slicked back dark hair and a pencil moustache, walking towards me having just entered the building; and I could see that he was wearing flashy rings and a gold necklace and watch. He looked to me a bit like a jeweller. For some reason he seemed to be familiar to me but being fifty miles away from home I couldn't work out where I'd seen him before, so I put it out of my mind.

I couldn't believe that when we got back to Maurice and Fred they had bought the Welsh dresser and luckily for me, with my little car already full, they were arranging with the dealer for it to be delivered the following week.

There was nothing there that Christine and I could afford to buy but we learned a lot by looking at the sort of things that were for sale and the prices they were fetching. After being there for a couple of hours I was ready for off and so was Fred, but Maurice wanted to stay. Christine decided to have a last wander round to look at the high-class jewellery stalls, while Fred and I grabbed a pot of tea and sat down at one of the tables provided where I could have a fag.

As I casually looked round for Christine I could see her talking to a man who had his back to me and he was with a stunning looking young lady. What a beauty, I thought. She had on a low-cut top and a tight fitting black skirt and was wearing high-heel stiletto shoes. I couldn't take my eyes off her. Just then the man turned around as Christine was walking away and I could see that it was 'Mr Spiv', the man who I had seen about an hour earlier. Christine got back to the table and, luckily for my wallet, she was empty handed and said, 'What a coincidence. I've just seen Steve who went to the same school as me when I was younger. He's here to buy a ring for his fiancé, I wish I could remember his second name.' I didn't hear her say the last bit as it hit me like a bolt of lightning where I'd seen him before. Six or seven months prior to this, my fellow detective John had been contacted by a snout, or informant, and we'd arranged to meet at the Cavendish night club in Sheffield where he pointed out to us 'Mr Spiv', now known to me as 'Steve the Spiv'; he was a travelling jeweller who used to go along to up-market jewellery shops with his classy girlfriend who was showing plenty of flesh. She would try on lots of expensive rings whilst pretending to be a prospective purchaser. This bamboozled the shop keepers and gave Steve the Spiv the chance to swap some of the real rings with cheap paste ones. The snout told us this because Steve the Spiv had just ripped off his sister and he wanted to get even. (Chapter 21, *What's Tha Up to This Time?*)

Jumping up, I glanced across the room again. Steve the Spiv and 'Marilyn Monroe' were looking closely at some of the rings in the jewellers' cabinets now. They'd been here for about an hour already, which meant to me that they hadn't made their move to switch anything or they would have already done a runner. They hadn't travelled all the way from Sheffield for nothing. If they were to be caught I'd need some help and quickly. Being off duty, I had no radio, so going outside I ran to a phone box and found the number for Harrogate police station, which I rang and asked to speak to a detective. Luckily there was one in the office and, after telling him who I was, and quickly relating the story, he said he was on his way and would be there in five or six minutes.

Before I left I'd told Christine that if Steve the Spiv left the building before I got back to discreetly follow them and get the number of the car they were driving. She didn't ask why, and I didn't have time to tell her, but she knew me well enough to know that there was a reason. The detective, whose name was Peter, arrived very quickly and, because I could see that the pair were still in the premises I explained further what their method of operation was and that we would keep an eye open from a distance. If we pounced too soon and nothing had been stolen, then we'd have blown the job. Something I'm sure would give us a clue. We would just have to wait and see.

When John and I had met the snout in Sheffield several months earlier he also mentioned to us that Steve the Spiv was selling his knocked-off gear to a shop owner in the city. It would be great to follow him back to Sheffield and catch him selling the stolen property, meaning that we could catch two birds with one stone: Steve the Spiv theft by deception, and his mate for handling stolen property. I couldn't take the risk of losing the opportunity of catching him today, so I made the decision to act now if the situation developed further.

As far as I can remember there were seven dealers of jewellery on the premises and the pair seemed to be flitting from one stall to the other and quickly. I whispered to Peter, 'I reckon it could be any time now. She's bending forward, giving the dealer a right "eye full" and he is losing patience and concentration as I can see her putting rings on and taking them off, she keeps flitting to other stalls and coming back again, which is totally confusing the dealers. For my money, Peter, any time now! Get ready pal.'

Sure enough two minutes later Marilyn Monroe seemed to stagger a little bit whilst holding her forehead and then she slowly crumpled to the floor. Steve the Spiv started to fan her with a newspaper while everybody gathered around to see if she was alright. Peter and I were at the scene in a flash and I heard Steve the Spiv say, 'Come on darling I'll take you outside, you need some fresh air, you'll soon be okay.' After which he gently helped her to her feet and slowly walked towards the door. Get ready. It was now or never time, right or wrong time and fingers crossed time.

As they went through the door and outside, Peter showed his warrant card whilst I stood behind him. They both looked startled and Marilyn Monroe seemed to come around very quickly and looked perfectly okay after her pretend fainting do. By this time Peter was joined by a plain-clothes police woman and the pair were separated from each other and detained.

Where was the evidence, if any that is? I went back inside and quickly asked that the jewellery stall holders check for any rings that might have been switched for paste ones. The deception would have happened in a flash and I was just hoping that we hadn't pounced too soon.

I wouldn't have known the difference between a proper diamond, ruby or emerald ring. To me they all looked like glass, but the jewellers themselves would know. You could have heard a pin drop in the jewellery quarter, as jewellers' loupes, or magnify glasses, were used to examine their stock. All we needed was one to be made of paste. After a few minutes it transpired that one of the seven dealers had been duped with one ring and the dealer where she had pretended to faint had had two rings switched. All three rings that had been switched were high carat diamonds and very valuable; and they were all found in Steve the Spiv's pocket when they were searched.

'Yes! Brilliant!' I said, and I was chuffed to bits. I turned to look at Christine, Maurice and Fred to tell them that I was going to Harrogate police station with Peter and the police woman and I explained why and that I would be back soon. All three of them looked surprised and didn't know what had happened until I told them, and I had to chuckle when Maurice said in his effeminate voice. 'What a lovely looking lad, what a shame he's with a woman.' It broke the tension and we all laughed.

Later, Peter went back to take statements from the jewellers concerned.

Steve the Spiv and Marilyn Monroe were now under arrest and when faced with the evidence, had no option but to admit to the crimes; and low and behold on the following Monday morning a jeweller in Harrogate rang the police station complaining that he also had had a ring switched on the Saturday, the same day that we were at the antique fair. They readily admitted to that as well. I also asked Peter if he would ask whether they had committed any more offences in the region in the hope that they would admit to John's snout's, sister's job; but without any evidence they wouldn't admit to any other jobs. For that reason, they were later charged and pleaded guilty at the Harrogate court. Unfortunately for us, and having no previous convictions, even though they must have done it dozens of times, they were both let off with a six-month suspended sentence.

Maurice and Fred were really impressed with the whole day's event and said that it was like taking part in a TV drama, playing cops and robbers, and even Fred, who was normally very quiet, didn't stop talking about it for ages.

Christine and I went to see them a couple of weeks later and the Welsh dresser fitted perfectly into their snug living room.

We knew Fred and Maurice for years and took them everywhere; and we learned a lot from them. A few years after that they both passed away. Firstly, Fred and then soon after Maurice. They had been together for many, many years and you could not talk or think about one without the other, they were like a married couple. Some time before they died they told Christine and me that they would leave their whole collection of antiques to Cannon Hall Museum in Barnsley and it was their dearest wish that the shop and house they owned at the corner of Church Street and Vicar Lane, just above where I was born, should be passed to the people of Darfield in order for it to be turned into the Maurice Dobson Museum.

Their wish came true and that little museum is there because of two extraordinary and interesting characters.

CHAPTER 6

Embarrassing or What?

The following Monday morning, at 9am, found me reporting for duty at West Bar police station in the middle of Sheffield. Including myself there were also eight policemen and one police woman from different police divisions within the Sheffield and Rotherham Force.

It was the obligatory police driving refresher course which we all had to take part in every few years. Some people found it a bind or unnecessary but, having been on a couple before, I enjoyed it and have always been grateful that I'd been taught by the best.

The course was being run by Sergeant David Hill and the other two instructors were PCs Ron Eveson and Don Caley, both highly experienced road traffic officers, as well as great guys.

Road safety, theory, forward thinking, practice, manoeuvrability and car sympathy were the ingredients of the course, as was us giving a running commentary when it was our turn to drive. This commentary allowed the instructor to know what we were observing and reacting to during the journey itself. It was quite intense as you had to make good progress but under no circumstance exceed the speed limit by even one mile per hour or you lost points.

It made a nice and welcome change from being a detective and all the paper work that we had to deal with, and so I decided to enjoy a week with a difference and learn as much as I could.

Three plain white Hillman Hunter cars were at our disposal, which meant that each car had an instructor and three officers. There was me, my good friend John Colley and a policewoman called Pat, and we were instructed by Don Caley. As a coincidence, Don later went on to marry Pat.

The course was to last a week and our first job each morning was to check the tyre pressures, oil, fuel and water levels in the radiator, as well as making sure that the car itself was spotless (I wish I'd not remembered that bit as I look outside at my filthy vehicle looking more like a shed than a car).

Correct driving is an art form in my opinion. Whether you're required to be quickly at the scene of an emergency, following a stolen car or on occasions when you are on surveillance and discretely following a suspect, you must have all your buttons on and know exactly what you are doing. Your priority is always safety-first both for yourself and the public. The reason for us to be on this refresher course in the first place was to hone our skills needed for when we were faced with any of those circumstances.

On each of the first four days we were to travel to different parts of the country taking it in turns to drive and commentate at the same time, whilst on the fifth day there was to be a written exam in the morning and manoeuvrability tests in the afternoon.

Before we set off, the instructors agreed that we should all meet up at dinner time at a designated meeting place, the separate routes to which having been decided by themselves earlier.

Ours was the first car to leave and Don gave us a specimen drive, including a commentary, as we went through the city and into Derbyshire and its beautiful countryside. An hour later we pulled up in a lay-by somewhere in Staffordshire for a chat. After lighting a fag, we all looked at each other and realized what was required of us. Don's driving skills, logic and attention to detail were incredible and it was nerve-racking to think that we had to 'follow that'. One of the things that Don said has stuck in my mind for ever and as we all know, almost all serious road accidents occur when someone has misjudged the overtaking manoeuvre and his words were, 'if in doubt, hang back'. Words that I apply to my own driving every day.

John went next followed by Pat, and by this time we were in a lay-by somewhere near Jodrell Bank Observatory in Cheshire. Our destination was a café behind Manchester Airport, which would take roughly an hour.

The first half an hour of Pat's commentary was okay, but as we got into the busier areas near Manchester it started to get a bit mixed up. She was a first-class policewoman and I'd worked with her on many occasions. She was a toughie alright, and when we had to deal with brawls in pubs she could certainly hold her own. As we got nearer to our destination you could see that she was sweating just like we all were, by being cooped up in the car for three and half hours. The concentration level we needed to commentate whilst driving was intense and nerve-racking at the same time. At some point Pat said, 'At the next roundabout I'm going to turn left – mirror, signal, now manoeuvre and then if there isn't a bloody loo around that corner I'm going to stop and get behind a hedge before I piss my pants.'

This comment cut the tension and we were all in hysterics and luckily for Pat we were literally three minutes away from the café. When we got there, she was out of that car like a flash, with her knees stuck together as she ran inside and disappeared into the loo. She was in full uniform and the people in the café thought there was a siege or something as she ran in.

I lit up a fag and we sat in the café waiting for Pat to return.

'What a relief that was,' Pat said as she joined us at the table. She took a bit of stick as we all had a laugh with her, but she gave back as good as she got.

Manchester airport wasn't as busy then as it is today, and because the café was very close to the runway, it was fascinating watching the planes landing and taking off while we had our snap.

After a large pot of tea and couple of fags, Don told me that it was my turn and I had to drive through Manchester from one side of the city to the other. Trust it to be my turn. It was so intense that I ended up sweating more than poor old Pat had.

I was instructed to follow the signs for the city centre, and then Middleton. I'd never seen as much traffic as there was in the centre of Manchester and as we got near to Middleton I remember seeing a sign for Heaton Hall, near to where a good friend of ours, Doris Turner, now lives. From there I was told to pick up the signs for Oldham and then follow the A635 road through Greenfield and up over Saddleworth Moor.

As we crossed Saddleworth Moor there was, at first, an odd sort of silence and even though I was supposed to be commentating, I just couldn't do it. We all understood what had taken place a few years before here: the horrendous torture, killing and then the burial of several innocent children. The words 'evil bastards' were used by us all as we thought about the despicable deeds committed by, what were then known as the Moors Murderers: Myra Hindley and her sadistic partner, Ian Brady. None of us could get our heads round how two people could conspire together to snare young, innocent children and commit such atrocities against them.

We stopped for a pot of tea and a fag in Holmfirth where the *Last of the Summer Wine* was to be filmed. Our mood still wasn't good at all and as Don drove us back to Sheffield, without commentating, we were all thinking and discussing those tragic events.

On the next day we ended up travelling through York, Malton and on to Filey, which was far more pleasant than the day before. The day after that we drove through Gainsborough, Lincoln and I can't remember whether it was Cleethorpes or Skegness where we ended up.

On the Thursday morning we swotted up on our theory ready for our exam which was to take place in the afternoon. We were all dreading it and especially me as my background in passing exams was useless. The results of the exam would be given on Friday afternoon after we'd completed our manoeuvrability tests on the old Lightwood Airbase at Norton in Sheffield.

I knew nothing about the history of the old airbase except that it had been used during the Second World War. On our arrival I could see several large Nissen huts near to what looked to have been an old marching or parade ground. On the far side of that was a long empty brick building which I assumed to have been the office block and canteen. Looking further I could see several roads with other smaller roads branching off them and I could only assume that they were where houses used to stand.

Pat and myself, along with one or two of the other lads were having a fag and a small pot of tea from the flasks that we'd been told to bring. The chat was all about the exams the day before and we all wondered if we had passed. Shortly afterwards the instructors shouted for us to bring the cars to another part of the airfield to the one we'd already seen. We then took it in turns to do the usual reverse parking, three-point turn and parallel parking, which was all straight forward. Each instructor gave points at what they had seen, and each team had been judged by the instructor from an opposing team.

That was it, we thought, we've done. Boy were we glad that it was all over. Just as we thought we'd finished Sergeant Hill called us back to the large parade ground where, what was initially a large empty space, was now full of large red and white traffic cones.

'Right everybody, you've all had a tough week and now you're at the last bit: the obstacle course. I'll show you how to negotiate it and then you'll have three practices each before you do the final run. The whole idea is to negotiate the course without knocking down a cone – it's a bit of fun really but still comprises part of your exam.'

Ron Eveson, the instructor, was holding a stop-watch and told us that the course had to be negotiated in one minute fifteen seconds.

When Sergeant Hill set off, Ron pressed the stop-watch button as he went around the course at an amazing rate of knots. It was awesome to see, and his final time was one minute, twelve seconds. Unbelievable.

Now it was our turn. We all thought that someone had lengthened the course because our times varied between one minute twenty and one minute thirty seconds, which we thought was very good.

'Now it's for real,' said the Sergeant, with a face that even a dog wouldn't lick.

It was exciting stuff and I can't remember in which order we went, but I had been chosen to be the last one. One by one each driver sped around the course. One or two were knocking the cones over, which got them a ten second penalty and the ones that didn't knock over the cones managed to get around the course in one minute, twenty seconds, and we all applauded each other's achievements.

My turn, here we go. Having had the fastest time of the group but also having knocked over two cones, I'd no chance, and Sergeant Hill's face was a study to see, he was full of himself and quite rightly so. As I started the car all the others were cheering me on. Before I started Don's words rang in my ears: 'If in doubt, hang back'. We'd all failed in the practice runs and I thought, bugger that – it's shit or bust, I'll give it my best shot.

I threaded the car through the cones and I heard the tyres squeal as I sharply swung to my right and before I knew it I was over the finishing line and I could see everyone else cheering and clapping as I came to a standstill. Had I hit a cone? I didn't know. Ron Eveson started with the first ones telling them their times and the number of cones, if any, that they had clipped. None had got the one minute, fifteen seconds, even though most had not hit a cone and I think the fastest time was one minute, seventeen seconds. Sergeant Hill was standing there with his arms folded and a huge grin of smug satisfaction on his face as Ron continued.

'The last one was you Johnson,' Ron said, as I held my breath. 'No cones clipped.' Up went a big cheer when he said 'Your time was – wait for it – one minute, eleven seconds. Congratulations, you've beaten the Sergeant by one second. You'd have thought we'd won the football pools as everyone was jumping up and down. Sergeant Hill was not amused. He had a face like an angry wasp and he strode over to the car that I had just driven and bent down to look at the tyres. Standing up again with a smile on his face he said, 'Don't get excited everybody. I heard his wheels squeal and I can see a scuff mark on Johnson's near side tyre which requires a five second penalty.'

Everyone went mad, including the other two instructors who were shouting at him, and he walked straight over to me, with a big smile on his face, 'Congratulations Johnson, I was only kidding, full credit due to you.' And then he addressed us all and shouted, 'You'll all be pleased to know that you have all passed your theory and practical tests. Well done to all of you.'

It certainly was a week with a difference. We'd all learned something and put it into practice. I was over the moon, not only for passing the exam which was a novelty, but for me to come top in the manoeuvrability test was incredible. Thanks for that lads, much appreciated, and I went home with a smile on my face.

Later I went for a few pints in the Mason's Arms, which was a few doors away from my home in Thorpe Hesley, and a few games of crib with Les, Harry and Wilf. What a good end to the night and I slept like a log.

Even though I knew that it was more by good luck than by good judgement that I'd beaten Sergeant Hill on the obstacle course, I was still chuffed to bits that I'd done it. Just to pass an exam, for me, was a novelty, but to come top was something else – a first and not such a pillock after all.

On the way to my sister's farm near to Outlane in Huddersfield, Christine told me that I'd been talking rubbish in my sleep: 'Mirror, signal, manoeuvre,' and then something about 'if in doubt hang back'. I couldn't stop laughing, fancy dreaming about it even after a week.

Just as we were passing the 'Wappy Spring' pub, near Crosland Moor and the farm, Christine suddenly shouted, 'Look at that over there. What is it?' On the pub car park was a yellow three-wheeler car, nothing unusual, you might think but this one was different though. I started to laugh as I remember Ricks reactions when we'd seen it last year in the same spot. (*What's Tha Playing at Nah?*)

It was an amazing sight which Christine hadn't seen before. On top of the yellow three-wheeler was a coffin, of all things, but sitting on top of the coffin was a dog wearing a crash helmet on its head – what a sight. The owner, a local character called Mangle Worzel, would be in the pub having a quick tipple as the day was a hot one.

The main reason for visiting the farm was to see our young nephew, Martyn, who was named after me. Farms can be busy places to work in and farm machinery can be very dangerous. He was only three years old and a couple of weeks earlier he had stuck his hand through the tiniest of holes in a metal safety plate which was surrounding the chain-driven motor of an elevator used for stacking bales of hay. Too late – his little fingers touched the chain and he lost the tips of two fingers. His mum and dad were obviously distraught, but apart from the tips of the fingers, he was okay. It had not affected any part of his life and he is now a big fine lad who's doing well for himself.

When we got to the farm my brother-in-law, John Beever, was already out in the fields and desperately trying to get the already stacked bales of hay back to the farm. The weather forecast for later that day was thunderstorms, high winds and heavy rain, which meant a panic to get the bales into a dry barn or they would be ruined. The fields that they were in were about half a mile away at the other side of the recently opened M62 motorway. As I set off at a brisk walk to them there wasn't a cloud in the sky, but the air was stuffy and humid. It was all hands-on deck; the forecast was obviously correct.

Just before I got to the first field I saw a Massey Ferguson tractor laden with bales of hay coming towards me. It was being driven by Jeremy Housley, a grand young lad. He slowed down and yelled out of the window, 'You've just come right Martyn, the storms over Manchester and heading our way. John and Alan Clough and his dad Harold are loading the other tractor – I'll be back in a bit,' and off he went.

Now at the field I helped the others to put bales onto the trailer and by the time we were done Jeremy was back again to load up the last tractor full of hay.

'Martyn, can you take the Massey tractor and trailer back to the farm, while we load up the last of the bales please?'

I loved driving tractors and I jumped at the chance. I trundled off towards the second field with the heavy load. In front of me I could see the open gateway between the five-foot-high drystone wall. Bloody hell that looks a narrow gap for the trailer to get through I thought to myself.

It was the first time that I'd driven anything with a large trailer on and to make matters worse, this one had a 10ft-high load on it. Scary, or what? Mirror, (there wasn't one), signal (I was in a field on my own there was no need) manoeuvre, here goes. I slowly managed to get the tractor and part of the trailer through the gap. The problem was that because of the length of the trailer I was now going to hit the stone wall at the other side of the road before I could make a turn, and traffic was building up on either side of me. I was cursing like a good 'un but managed to reverse back through the gateway and into the field. The second go was worse than the first and

I managed to get the trailer with its precarious load trapped on the edge of the gatepost. Embarrassing, or what?

I'd just come top in a manoeuvrability test and there I was stuck in a bloody gateway. I was as 'nazy as a crab's arse'.

Just then I saw John coming towards me with a young calf hanging around his neck. I was frustrated and angry with myself and must have used a thousand swear words in the space of five minutes as I told John that I was well and truly stuck. To make matters worse it had started to rain heavily.

'Right Martyn, you grab the calf and I'll deal with the trailer. I know it's not easy. One of the cows has just given birth to this calf in the field. We're bringing the herd in for them to be milked. The calf obviously can't walk and needs to be in some dry straw before he gets wet through.'

So, I grabbed the calf from John, which was covered in after-birth and blood, put him around my shoulders with his four feet hanging over my chest and set off to the farm. Passers-by were looking at me in amazement as I walked down Crossland Road and joined Lindley Moor Road and then right over the bridge of the M62 to the farm. The poor little calf wasn't happy at all and was weeing all down my back; and then to make matters worse John then passed me with the fully laden tractor that I should have been driving – how the hell had he done that when I couldn't. I felt a proper twerp.

Back at the farm, I put the calf in the barn and wrapped him in straw where he would be both warm and dry.

The other trailer had also returned to the farm followed by the herd of cows driven by Alan and his dad Harold. Luckily the calf was alright and a few minutes later when he was united with his mum in the barn he was suckling like a good 'un. I stripped off in the barn and hosed off all the cow-shit, after-birth and wee before I got dressed again. My sister, Bronnie, had hurriedly made a lovely meal, after which we braved the fearsome storm as we headed home.

My youngest son, Paul, who was born several years later, loved helping his Uncle John on the farm along with his cousin, James. They both went into agriculture on leaving school and even to this day they are both working in farming.

Paul is also a good cricketer and, being a big lad, he can hit a ball a long way. Because he worked on the local farm in Wentworth his team mates called him the 'Cow-shit Kid,' and when he used to go into bat you could hear spectators shouting, 'Come on Cow-shit, let's have a few sixes,' which made me laugh.

⋆   ⋆   ⋆

This chapter is in memory of my fellow driver on the driving course – Pat Vaughan who later married and became Pat Caley – also thanks to you Don for teaching me how to drive anything properly except, perhaps, a tractor and trailer!

CHAPTER 7

What Next? You NEVER knew

One day I was upstairs in the CID office typing up a report using both my index fingers. The amount of paperwork required for a court case used to send us all barmy. I was a detective not a typist, and my job was to catch criminals, which I didn't have the time to do because of bloody paperwork. What a ball-aching carry on.

I'd had enough and lit yet another fag and at the same time I picked up my pint pot of tea only to find it was empty. Looking around me I could see both Rick and John from our team – also typing away – so I went to mash us all another pot full.

The old stone Victorian and soot-covered nick on Whitworth Lane was situated in the industrial east end of Sheffield and was surrounded by smoke-belching steel works. Where there's muck, there's brass – and where there's brass, there's always somebody trying to nick it. Sheffield was the steel and cutlery capital of the world in those days. It was mainly stolen scrap brass or other types of metal that we were on the look out for, as well as the people who had stolen it. It was a tough area to work and we were all kept busy.

Brass, where I come from, also means 'money or cash'. Just after I'd finished typing my report the sergeant in the main office phoned to tell me that a lady was downstairs and was wanting to talk to me. Before I went I checked in the mirror – it could be a nice leggy blonde, about twenty-five with a nice figure, I thought, so I straightened my tie and combed my hair.

As I entered the waiting room I could see that I'd wasted my time. Standing in front of me was a medium-built lady of about sixty with a well-tanned, leathery-looking face and she looked really agitated and upset. She was wearing a floral silk scarf around her head, a brightly-coloured shawl wrapped round her body and a long woollen dress down to her ankles. As I introduced myself I had the feeling that I'd met her somewhere before but couldn't work out where until she told me her name and where she lived.

A couple of years prior to this and when I was in uniform, I'd driven the Panda car up to the top of Piggy Lane, near to High Hazel's Park and then onto the gypsy encampment.

I was often up there for various reasons but mainly looking for people who were 'wanted' or to serve a summons on them. It was always the same when I got there. I'd say 'Is _____ here? I've got an arrest warrant for him.' The replies went, 'he's not here sir... never heard of him, sir ... doesn't live here, sir' or '...maybe he's dead, sir'.

When you don't know what the man you're looking for looks like it was nigh on impossible to make an arrest.

Just as I was leaving the gypsy site on that day there was a right commotion coming from outside of one of the older type caravans and a lady ran out of the door. I turned to look, and she was shouting to me. 'Help us, please sir, help us – please.' It was the lady I was now talking to in the waiting room. 'My daughter is pregnant, and her waters have broken. Can you call for an emergency ambulance please?'

I could hear her daughter screaming with pain, and her mum ran back to the caravan in a panic. Police radios in those days were fairly new and unreliable and had to be charged up every few hours; and just as I got through to the office the battery died on me. (If only someone had invented mobile phones!) I won't repeat what I said at that point. The poor girl's screams were louder now and coming more often and it was obvious that the baby was well on its way. There was no one else around to help but me and, although I'd helped cows and pigs to give birth on the farm, I didn't relish the idea of helping with the birth of something more important – that needed a professional and bloody quick.

'Grab her things love. Don't worry I'm taking you to hospital,' I shouted, as I reversed the police car up to the caravan door. I jumped out and pushed the passenger seat as far back as possible to make room for the daughter. Her mum and I managed to get her into the passenger seat and mum, climbed into the back with her daughter's clothes. Would we make it on time? The thoughts of me having to deliver a baby were daunting to say the least.

Blue light on, we set off to the Northern General and on the way I discovered that the old lady's name was Tutti and the daughter was Amanda. A journey of about four miles with the blue light flashing would normally take minutes but this one, because of the pressure, seemed to take hours and I was sweating like a pig. Amanda's screams were ear piercing and came closer together. I knew that the birth was getting very near.

At last we arrived outside the hospital and I ran in to fetch someone. With a huge sigh of relief, I was able to pass on the responsibility to the hospital staff who immediately rushed her off with her mum running behind her. I didn't know who needed gas and air most – her or me – but I lit a fag anyway.

I didn't see them both again, that is until now when I was talking to Tutti in the general office of the Attercliffe nick.

'How's your daughter and baby going on Tutti?'

'They're okay thanks to you. The baby girl arrived only about ten minutes after you dropped us off at the hospital. But it's my son I want to talk to you about. He's turned out to be an evil pig of a man and I need your help again. Please, please, sir, help us.'

'Go on Tutti. What's the problem, love?' I could see that she was really upset, and she began to sob.

'Sir, sir. You are a good man and helped us. My daughter remembered your name and, as you know, gypsies don't grass on anybody. Both my husband, daughter and myself are worried sick that my son is going to kill someone before he's done.'

'What do you mean?'

'He travels up and down the country and hasn't lived with us for the last three years. We know that he's breaking into houses of rich old ladies and torturing them until they tell him where their brass is. If he was only stealing things I wouldn't tell you, sir, but he needs to be caught before somebody dies. I don't know where he is because he lives out on the road, but please, please catch him, sir. Thieving is one thing, but we've not brought him up to torture old ladies.'

She gave me what details she had, including his name and date of birth.

'Bless you, sir, I know I can trust you to help us again.' Then off she went, sobbing.

That was a first, we often got tip-offs from the criminal fraternity about someone they had a grudge against, but I'd never had one from the traveller community. It was unheard of, but also understandable, given what Tutti had told me. This scumbag needed catching and quickly.

Thanks for that Tutti, I thought as I went back upstairs – time to think about what action to take over a pint pot of tea and a fag. There were no rich women in Attercliffe for sure, or they wouldn't be living in back-to-back or terraced houses, so I had to spread my area of search.

I contacted the Crime Intelligence Unit at Force Headquarters and asked them to check their records to see if there were any violent crimes against women outstanding. I also gave them an update on our man, 'Mr Spineless Bastard' and gave them a description: full name and date of birth, white male, 5'10", dark hair, green eyes and of medium build, last seen in the Sheffield area several months ago when he was driving a newish white Transit van and towing a new flashy white caravan with fancy windows (he wouldn't have been able to buy that with the proceeds of stolen scrap metal). I also asked them to register my interest in him and wanted to interview him if he turned up anywhere in the future; to which they replied that they would record that now and contact the national computer people in Scotland Yard.

Knowing that Mr Spineless Bastard was now officially wanted for questioning, there was nothing else we could do but wait for any developments.

After work, Rick and I decided that a quick pint in Mucky Mary's would finish off the day nicely. Tucked away in the backstreets of the east end of the city the little pub looked more like an end of terrace house than a pub. It only had two small rooms and just outside the front door was a red telephone box with a pane of glass missing from the door.

'ONE, TWO, THREE, CID' was our usual greeting when we visited the pub, followed by being blown kisses from the male prostitutes who were in the snug. In the other room were the female prostitutes and, being Saturday night, it was always busy for them; they were dressed up to the nines and ready for business.

'Hi, big boy. I'll bet you've got a big truncheon,' said Maureen, one of the new girls, and she then pulled my head forward until it was between her ample bosom. When I came up for air Cecil, the barman, passed me a pint, paid for by Doreen, one of the lads in the Snug. He was jokingly looking daggers at Maureen and I had to laugh at what he said next: 'I want him first darling,' and he pouted his lips and blew me a kiss from the other room.

'Phone for Maureen,' shouted Cecil as he came in from outside the pub.

Then the girl who fancied my truncheon left by the front door. I couldn't stop laughing as I remembered the first time that Rick had taken me in there some two years previously. He never told me a thing about what to expect. On that occasion and after hearing, 'One, two, three CID,' as we entered the pub, George, with the long blonde wig, blew me a kiss and called me 'Sweetie'. Rick was in hysterics looking at my face and he had to grab me before I flattened him.

The carry-on in the pub was all new to me then but now I knew the score, things were very different. I knew what would happen next and it did. The front door opened again and back in came Maureen. 'Another client – I'm off to the flat, see you in an hour, bye,' and off she went with a smile on her face.

A few minutes later it happened again. Cecil the barman left the pub, then a minute later came back in. 'Phone for you 'Soft Cock',' who then left only to come back in, in an excited state two minutes later.

'Woo, he sounds really sweet, and my first customer of the night – see you in about an hour,' and off he went giggling to himself.

When I'd seen this strange behaviour when Rick first took me into the pub I couldn't understand it. When Cecil shouted 'phone,' for whoever it might be, they would leave the building only to happily return a couple of minutes later to say cheerio. What was that all about, I'd thought to myself, I hadn't heard a phone ring, so what was going off?

I asked Rick, my mate, who had been using the pub for several years before me.

'I'm glad you're confused pal, because I bloody was when I first came across it,' and he laughed and pointed to the door of the pub, 'at the other side of that door, which is not very thick as you can see, stands the telephone kiosk.' A pane of glass has been removed from the kiosk, which means that when the phone rings it can be heard from inside the pub.'

'Right – but why does someone inside the bloody pub go and answer the phone? Tell me that mate, I'm still baffled.'

'Both the girls and the lads have regular clients, who each have the number of the telephone box, so if the clients want a quick shag, they know that they'll be in the pub awaiting a call for business.'

I couldn't believe what I was hearing, no wonder I was confused.

'Why don't they ring the pub itself then?'

'They can't because Mary won't let them in case she gets in trouble with us, the law. She doesn't mind them being in here at all, where they are safe and warm, rather than them walking the streets where they're open to danger when they're looking for clients. Mary's a lovely woman and genuinely cares for them, but neither is she daft. It's only a little pub and while ever they're in here they're spending money which keeps the pub going. That way, everybody's happy.'

Rick had just finished telling me the story when, blow me, I could hear the phone ringing outside and Cecil ran out. When he came back in seconds later he said, 'Call for you Mr Johnson.' I nearly dropped bow legged. Who the hell could that be? I certainly hoped that they weren't looking for any business from me.

As I left I was scratching my head and wondering who it could possibly be. Everyone was cheering. On picking up the phone I heard John's voice who we'd left at the nick typing.

'I've phoned Mary's private number upstairs. Her husband's in a bad way, as you know, and she's nursing him, so she gave me the kiosk number so that I could talk to you there.'

'What's up John?'

'Don't know, but the Detective Superintendent and the Detective Chief Inspector want to see you if you're nearby. Doesn't sound serious though.'

'Thanks John, I'm with Rick. I'll be back in about fifteen minutes.'

On re-entering the pub everyone was laughing and wondering who'd been ringing me on 'THE WORKS' phone. I told Rick who the call was from and what it was about, so he supped the last of his beer and we were off. Just for a laugh I blew a kiss into both rooms and shouted, 'Going to the office, back in an hour.' The place was in uproar with laughter. What a great bunch of people they were.

We were back at the nick in about ten minutes and I was a bit nervous. It wasn't every day that you were called to a meeting with the two 'top dogs'. My mind was working overtime wondering if I'd done something wrong, but I couldn't come up with anything.

The two gaffers were upstairs in the inspector's office and called me in and told me to sit down. A good sign, I thought.

'Have I done something wrong, sir?'

'No Johnson,' the boss replied, 'there's just one or two questions we want to ask you. When did you pass your sergeant's exam?' they asked.

'I've not passed my sergeant's exam sir, I haven't even taken it. It's not what I want to do.' At which point they looked at each other and I could see that they were both surprised.

'What do you think of _____?' (A detective who worked on one of the other teams).

'He's a good bloke sir and gets on with us all and in my opinion a good detective, sir.'

'Do you like working in the CID?'

'Yes and no, sir. I didn't ask to go into CID, I was told to do so. There's far too much paperwork for my liking, which stops you being out catching criminals. I also miss working a beat and working with the public if I'm totally honest.'

'Okay Johnson, thanks for being honest about that, but we thought you'd passed your sergeants exam,' they said, as they both looked at each other and shrugged their shoulders.

It was a strange meeting, more of a convivial chat than an interview, and the officers didn't seem to want anything specific. A few other questions about nothing in particular were asked, and after about ten minutes, I was informed that they had got someone else to see; and that that was all they wanted and thanked me. I left the office scratching my head. What the hell was that all about?

Fifteen minutes later, at the end of my shift, I was on my way home and mulling things over. What a day. What next? We never knew.

CHAPTER 8

One Pillock
After Another

The Monday morning shift was always busy down the 'Cliffe'. It was a massive division to cover and contained nearly all the industrial part of the city. The tens of thousands of workers tended to live near to their place of work, usually in long rows of terraced houses with outside toilets and no bathrooms. It was estimated that about 500 tons of soot from coal fires and furnaces were deposited onto the streets of Attercliffe every year. Many people chewed gum to stop their mouths clogging up. Taking a bath was a family occasion and taken in a long zinc-coated, metal bathtub which, when not in use, was hung by a nail on the outside wall of the house. All the hot water for the bath had to be heated on either the gas stove or coal fire. First in were the children of the house, followed by mum. Lastly was the man of the house who, because of the nature of his physical work, was the dirtier one. With the use of a block of carbolic soap and a scrubbing brush his wife would scrub him clean.

Clothes-washing days were always on a Monday down the Cliffe, when the steelworks shut down for a few hours, and every cobbled street had clothes lines strung from one side of the street to the other for them to hang the washing on to dry. There was no such thing as central heating and ice used to form on the insides of all the windows in wintertime, causing everyone in the house to huddle around the fire.

Inevitably, with such a big area to police, and with all the thousands of people who lived there, crimes were committed. People would go out for a few hours to visit their parents, only to come back to find that their house had been broken into. Shops were also broken into, push bikes were stolen as sometimes were cars. All would be reported on a Monday morning which is why, as detectives, we were so busy at the nick. The crime scene had to be visited and the finger print department sent for to check the scene for prints in the hope that they could be matched up with a known criminal, statements had to be taken from complainants, and crimes recorded in our diaries later to be investigated. At times it could be bedlam and annoyingly to me all that took time away from us going out and finding the culprits.

On this occasion both Rick and I were using the same brown Morris Minor CID car and taking it in turns to visit the different crime scenes. It was the usual stuff: a few housebreakings on the rough Manor Estate and one or two in Wincobank. At different sites, scrap metal was stolen as were several bikes. Like the push bikes that had been stolen, scrap metal could be sold very quickly so that we wouldn't catch the thieves with the goods. So, Rick and I both decided that we should check out the local scrap-metal yards first of all, which we did, but unfortunately with no success. It was also the same when we checked out the local second-hand shops and they all said the same thing that they'd had no bikes offered for sale.

By then it was almost dinner time, so we went back to the nick for our snap and a pot of tea. A large ham and tomato sandwich plus two bananas, followed by a pot of tea and a fag made me feel better, and we were ready for off again on our enquiries. Halfway down the stairs from the CID office the inspector shouted me back.

'I was busy doing an interview, Martyn, when you first came in for your snap. Can you ring 'Detective Sergeant Bloggs' at the Hull City Police Force? He's got something that might be of interest to us.'

I hadn't a clue why I had to ring the police in Hull, so I made the call which was answered by the Detective Sergeant himself.

I introduced myself and he sounded quite excited.

'Hi Martyn, thank you for ringing me back,' he said, and then he went on to tell me that in the early hours of that morning a silent alarm went off at a fairly large house on the outskirts of Hull. Apparently, there was a ten-minute audible delay on the alarm system so two of the Hull patrol cars were sent to the job. Just as they got to the big metal gates of the property a white Transit van flew out of the drive and deliberately smashed into one of the police cars, injuring one of the officers and then speeding off. As he told me that, and at the mention of a white Transit van, I crossed my fingers in the hope that it might be Tutti's son, Mr Spineless Bastard.

He went on and said that the driver of the other police car broadcast the vehicle's details over the radio and asked for an ambulance to attend the scene at the same time. A little while after this the van was stopped and the male occupant arrested. He was in possession of several thousand pounds in cash and some expensive jewellery. When other officers and the patrol car went to the house concerned, they found that the house had been broken into and inside they found that an old lady had been tied up to a chair and her mouth had been gagged. Her nose was bleeding, one of her cheeks had been cut with a knife, and there were two cigarette burns on her chest. The sergeant said that she was in a terrible state and had to be rushed to the hospital suffering from burns and trauma. The evil bastard had tortured her until she had given him the combination to a safe that was found open in the next room.

'We've been in touch with National Intelligence and discovered that you want to interview him as well. Can you come over?'

'Can I come over? I'd crawl there on my hands and knees if I knew that he was Mr Spineless Bastard himself.'

After speaking to the sergeant again I discovered that it was indeed the same man and I found myself bunching up my fist at the thought of what this evil person had done.

Tutti was right in contacting me, he could have killed the poor lady, and after getting the nod from the boss, Rick and I set off to Hull. There were no motorway networks leading to Hull in those days, so off we went through Rotherham, Doncaster, Hatfield and Thorne. Just before Goole was Boothferry Bridge which was made of thick wooden boards that rattled loudly when you crossed. As a nipper if we went on a club trip to Bridlington the bus used to go over that bridge and it used to terrify me, and my mum used to have to cover my ears, or I'd cry.

Just before we got to Hull you could see, to our right, an absolutely huge steel structure rising from the waters of the mighty River Humber. This structure, over the next few years, would morph into an engineering masterpiece. At 7,280ft long and 510ft high, the Humber Bridge is truly amazing. Now vehicles can travel the length of the east side of England in more or less a straight line, thus saving hundreds of miles and fuel.

Hull looked to be a beautiful city and even though the Detective Sergeant was out taking a statement from the driver of the police car and the lady herself at the hospital, we were made very welcome. On his return he told us that the police-car driver had sustained a broken collar bone and had broken his right leg. The lady, although traumatized, was going to be okay. He also told us that since our phone call, the traveller caravan had been traced to a site about ten miles away from the scene of the incident. The forensic lads were there going through both the van and caravan to see what else they could find.

Mr Spineless Bastard was in the cell and had had no option but to admit to doing the robbery as he had been found in possession of the property stolen from the old lady's house. I told the sergeant that my information was that he had done other similar jobs before the one that he had now been captured for.

As I entered his cell, along with the sergeant, you could somehow feel the evilness emanating from him, and as I pictured the old lady tied to a chair and then being burnt with a cigarette, I could have cheerfully smashed him to a pulp, as I am sure you who are reading this, could have done. As I sat opposite him at the table I leaned forward and lit a cigarette – I couldn't help myself as I slowly pushed the lit end of my cigarette towards him. As I got nearer to him there was a look of terror on his face as he thought that he was going to get some of his own medicine. Both the sergeant and I knew that I wasn't going to do anything stupid with the cigarette and I slowly and deliberately stubbed my cigarette out in the ashtray and then left the cell.

People who have been caught committing crimes such as this and knowing that they were going to be sent to prison for a long time, would confess to having committed other crimes prior to the one they had been charged with. These crimes would then be taken into consideration by the judge when passing a sentence. Knowing this, he'd already admitted to several other jobs but none of which cleared any crime up in the Sheffield area.

The sergeant invited us to have a meal with him in the canteen and asked us if we would like some fish straight from the docks to take home. We didn't need asking twice as we both loved fish and shortly after the sergeant had made a phone call, a chap arrived with a box containing fresh haddock fillets which cost half the price that we would have had to pay at the Sheffield Wholesale Market. What a bonus.

The following morning, I visited the gypsy camp in Sheffield. Tutti was distraught when I told her what her son had done to the old lady, but she was also more than thankful for the fact that he had been arrested, and as she quite rightly said, the shock could have killed the poor woman.

When I got back to the nick Inspector Hepworth wanted to see me, so I went to his office.

Sitting with him in his office with a cup of tea was a chap of about 35, dressed in an immaculate suit with a silk handkerchief peeping out of his breast pocket. I also noticed that he was wearing several rings on both hands and a chunky gold chain on one of his wrists – he looked a proper 'spiv'. The inspector introduced him as being a detective called Peter from the Metropolitan Police Force in London. Apparently, he had travelled up to Sheffield to make an arrest of a van driver who had committed some offence or other in their area.

'Right, sir, but what am I here for?'

At which stage Peter piped up with a strong Cockney accent, 'I thought the geezer I'm after was in this division of Sheffield, but I've now been told that he's somewhere in Barnsley, so the inspector suggested that I contact you, being a Barnsley man, to help me find him.'

What a weird coincidence, I thought, two 'out of Sheffield' enquiries in two days and I wondered what this one would bring.

'Right, Peter, where do we begin? What details have you got?'

'Not much really. His name and his last place of work, which is where I've just visited, and they've told me that they sacked him a couple of weeks ago and he's now working at a factory somewhere in Barnsley. That's it, all I've got to go on.'

'What was the factory that he got sacked from?' I asked, and he gave me the details. He was lucky because I knew Dave the manager of the factory from when I was on the beat and I'd sometimes call in for a pot of tea with him, so I gave him a call.

'Hi Dave, I understand that you've just sacked a lad from your spot and I've got a detective here looking for him. I need to find out where in Barnsley he's working. Any ideas?'

'I know exactly where he's working Martyn, but that so-called detective was pig ignorant and a pain in the arse, so I wasn't going to tell him anything.'

'Thanks for that, Dave. I owe you a pint pal.'

As we set off to Barnsley I could tell that Peter was full of himself and his own importance. Now I knew what Dave meant, he was suffering from 'I' disease – I this, I that and I the other! He never stopped 'brawnging' as we say in Barnsley; and never shut up about how their police force was the best and without saying it out loud, he was inferring that all us northern bobbies were country bumpkins. After half an hour of it I knew that my feelings about him were right – another word we used in Barnsley fitted him to a tee – he was a first class PILLOCK.

On arrival at the factory we soon found the man he was after and he was then handcuffed and put in the back seat with the detective. From there we drove to the charge office in Sheffield, where Peter the detective was going to place him in custody until he got further instruction from his boss.

Job done, and I was glad to be rid of him. I wouldn't trust him as far as I could throw him.

Country bumpkin one – Detective Spiv none, I thought to myself as I drove back to the nick, signed off duty and went home after first nipping into the Mason's Arms at Thorpe Hesley for a couple of pints and a game of crib with my mates.

The following morning when I arrived for work, I was just about to mash when I was collared by the inspector – what this time? I thought.

This is what he told me. Apparently after I'd dropped Peter the Spiv off at the charge office and after the prisoner was placed in the holding cell, Peter had asked to use the phone to ring his boss in London. Ten minutes later, having told the office sergeant that he had another enquiry to make he left the building.

'You must be joking, sir,' I said, 'what enquiries? He's already got his prisoner.'

'Hang on Martyn – get this then,' said the inspector. 'You'll not believe it. The typist in the office heard the call being made to his boss.'

'Go on, sir, I'm all ears.'

'Listen to this. The typist heard him say quite clearly: 'I like it up here guv, and if you let me stay the night, I'll give you a case of that stolen whisky that we recovered last week.' Then he paused and continued by saying: 'Thanks guv.'

I couldn't believe what I was hearing as the inspector continued his account. 'A prisoner in the cells and a missing detective was all that the charge office sergeant needed, and he contacted our superintendent. He in turn got in touch with the Met and told them what had happened in no uncertain terms. They obviously weren't best pleased and immediately despatched two police vehicles containing high ranking officers up to Sheffield.'

I was dying to speak but couldn't get a word in, so our inspector continued: 'Low and behold, shortly before their arrival, the detective himself arrived back at the charge office in a state of intoxication. He was, apparently, as drunk as a skunk and demanded that the prisoner was released to him. The sergeant obviously refused and locked the detective up and put him in a cell, where he was shouting obscenities. Apparently the "big cheeses" from the Met arrived and were full of apologies to our boss. They weren't pleased at all and later took both the prisoner and the detective away with them in separate vehicles. What a disgusting and disgraceful carry on.'

I'd been wanting to speak and ask questions but now I couldn't speak and couldn't believe what I'd heard. What happened to Peter the spiv detective after that I've no idea but I would like to think that he got the sack. Nobody could believe it, but I can assure you it is true, and it was the talk between us all for several weeks.

I'd been right, Peter the detective was a first-class PILLOCK.

Unfortunately, the Metropolitan Police Force was having problems at the time culminating in several of their officers being dismissed for various reasons. That was a long time ago and luckily, they've put all that behind them.

Note: A few months after the arrest of Tutti's son, I saw her again and she told me that the family had disowned him and that she had been told that he'd been sent to prison for twelve years. Once more she thanked me profusely for helping her.

CHAPTER 9

Comedy of Errors

Both Christine and I, as well as our kids Richard and Sally, were all excited. Police wages in those days weren't as good as they are today, but Christine had managed to save up some of her family allowance money ready for our annual holidays.

Annual holidays at our house in those days usually consisted of a day here and a day there because that's all we could afford with having kids and a mortgage.

Living at the other side of the city to us was Rick Hardwick, my detective partner at work, his wife Doreen and children Paul and Tracy who were a bit older than our kids. They were our best friends and we were all going on holiday together. Apart from Rick being a first-class detective he was also a brilliant, self-taught artist. He was that good and his paintings in such great demand that people bought them before they were even dry. At 3ft x 2ft, he sold them for £7 fully framed, what a bargain.

Rick had a Ford Capri and I had an old Ford Escort which sometimes struggled, so a good pal of mine, Curly Hutchinson, had loaned me his new Ford Corsair, what a treat. Neither Rick or I had driven anywhere down south before, never mind to St Ives in Cornwall. We'd been told that it was about 350 miles away and, because of the lack of motorways in those days, it would be about a 12-hour drive. What a load of rubbish, we'd looked at the map – down to Mansfield and then pick up the A38 road to Bodmin in Cornwall – a piece of cake, or so we thought – MISTAKE number 1.

MISTAKE number 2. We hadn't realized how many other people would be leaving the north and also heading south on a Saturday morning in the school holidays.

MISTAKE number 3. When you've been stuck in a traffic jam for an hour and then when it starts to move again, why do the ladies in both cars want a toilet? After setting off again, Sally, our youngest, needed to be fed and nappy changed.

MISTAKE number 4. Why did we forget the bloody headache tablets? My head was spinning. After nine hours of twists, turns and 'are we there yet, dad?' every two minutes and stopping and starting, we all pulled into a lay-by somewhere near Bristol. We got out of our cars and the air was blue, with both fag smoke and obscenities. We were all knackered, and I'm sure that you also know the feeling.

After studying the map again, we decided to push on and try to get as far as Taunton in Somerset and stay there for the night. We'd also heard of Somerset cider and scrumpy and a couple of hours later we found a cosy little pub and booked in for the night. Neither Rick or I were cider drinkers, preferring instead good old beer. When trying to get information out of a villain in a pub you had to be able to cope with more than a few pints of the amber liquid and both of us could handle it.

With the kids in bed and wives having a natter, Rick and I went to the bar and ordered a pint of cider apiece. The landlord smilingly told us that it could only be served by the glass as it was so strong. Rick and I looked at each other in amazement, ordered two glasses and knocked them back fairly quickly. We should have listened to the landlord – but we didn't.

MISTAKE number 5 was on its way.

Was it strong stuff? No idea.

How many glasses did we have? No idea.

What time did we leave the bar? No idea.

What was breakfast like? No idea.

What time did we surface? No idea.

Would we drink cider again? Never ever, ever, ever again.

Were we in trouble with our wives? Erm, erm oh yes! I suppose you could say that.

Apparently, I surfaced at about 2pm and Rick a couple of hours later. Both of us had hangovers big style, and much to the displeasure of our wives, we both knew that driving was out of the question. We had no option but to stay another night at the pub (but alcohol free). We felt really rough and we had to wait until the following afternoon before we felt well enough to set off and drive the rest of the way to St Ives.

The journey there was in stony silence. What should have been a 12-hour drive from Sheffield took us nearly THREE days. Could it get any worse? I asked myself.

What a beautiful place St Ives was, but it looked as if the whole of Yorkshire had gone on holiday at the same time as us. St Ives was full, but it was a lovely day, the sun was shining, and luckily after a while we were able to find two separate bed and breakfast places to stay not far from the harbour.

The following morning after breakfast, pushchair, beach towels, sunscreen, nappies, etc at the ready we set off to have a look round. It was another red-hot day and as we reached one of the several beaches, we walked on the promenade to find a nice spot where we could settle down for a day in the sun.

MISTAKE number 6. The promenade was about 4ft higher than the beach when suddenly I saw a woman sunbathing topless – what a beauty, you don't see that every day! Blimey, I'd never seen a topless sunbather before and neither had Rick after I nudged him. I was gawping that much at her that I lost my footing and ended up going 'arse over tit' over the edge of the promenade, landing on the beach almost next to the gorgeous woman. Embarrassing, or what? I wasn't amused, unlike the rest of the gang and other spectators who had seen what had happened and were looking down at me and laughing hysterically. They didn't let me live that one down! What a twerp.

It was no wonder that so many people made the long journey to St Ives, it was quite simply incredible. With beautiful coves, soft sand, warm blue seas, cosy cottages and quaint shops it provided us with plenty to do and see in this paradise of a place. Rick was in his element – somewhere near to the harbour was an arcade containing various artists' studios who were all painting and selling their stunning works. I couldn't even draw a straight line, but Rick was engrossed with them, spending several hours every day just watching. His favourite artist was, as far as I can remember, called Keith English. Neither Rick or I could be serious for long, we both loved a laugh and a bit of 'kid and soft', but when he was watching Keith paint he was in another world.

We'd sensibly (for a change) decided to travel back home on Sunday afternoon in the hope that we'd miss all the weekend traffic that we'd experienced the week before. Leaving Rick at the artists' studios, the rest of us went down to the beach for our last bit of sunbathing and a dip in the sea with the kids.

A brass band was playing down on the quayside near the lifeboat station and everyone was singing along, it was brilliant.

Christine is a very strong swimmer and along with Doreen and the kids they went down to the sea while I looked after the deck chairs and bits and bobs. I'd just bought a cracking Cornish pasty, but I'd only taken two bites when a bloody seagull snatched it out of my hands.

Both the beach and the sea were full of people, it was red hot, when suddenly, we all heard someone scream at the top of their voice: 'SHARK!' Everyone jumped up, including me, and ran to the water's edge to where our kids were swimming. Talk about panic. At the word shark, everyone else joined in until the entire water's edge was full of people rescuing their children. Some were pointing out to sea, kids were scrambling out of the water, parents were panicking, and I could hear Christine still shouting, 'shark! Get out! Get out!'

A lifeguard appeared from nowhere and after running into the sea and seeing the 'shark' he explained to Christine and everyone else in a loud voice that it was, in fact, a DOLPHIN.

MISTAKE number 7. Christine's face, who had been the first one to shout, was bright red, some people were laughing, and others were crying with relief that their children were safe and not in any danger. The guard went on to explain to Christine, who by this time was feeling very, very embarrassed, that 'jaws' was in fact, a dolphin called Beaky who visited several harbours in the summer months. What a bloody carry on. Thank goodness it was Christine that had made that mistake and not me.

After changing back at the digs, we were ready for off, and luckily the traffic conditions were far different to the ones on our way down.

Christine had a fascination with Daphne du Maurier's book called *Jamaica Inn* and whilst Rick and Doreen went on their way we did a small detour to visit the pub itself. It was also a handy toilet break and off we went once more, heading for home.

Somewhere or other, I'm not sure where, I was driving along the road and in a split second the sky turned jet black followed by something hitting the windscreen. I slammed the breaks on as I couldn't see a thing. What the hell had happened, I didn't know and jumped out of the car. The kids were screaming, and Christine was in a blind panic. As I quickly looked around me I could see several other cars behind us that had also pulled up and their windscreen and cars were also covered in black. What the hell was that? Looking closer I couldn't believe my eyes. Mine must have been the first car to be hit, followed by the others and as I looked more closely I could see that the cars were covered with tens of thousands of honeybees. What a sight, we'd obviously run into a huge swarm. Luckily, everyone was alright apart from the occupants of one car who had been driving with their windows partially open because of the heat and they had been badly stung. MISTAKE number 8 (for the bees that is).

That was the first time that any of us had seen a swarm of bees and especially one so huge. It was pitiful to see, there were dead and dying bees everywhere. After we had brushed the bees off the car we set off again. That was over forty years ago and it's weird because since that time we've seen several other large swarms of honeybees as, for the past twenty-odd years, Christine has been the local beekeeper and she keeps her honeybees in the grounds of Wentworth Woodhouse, the longest-fronted country house in the British Isles and made famous by our friend Catherine Bailey's bestselling book *Black Diamonds*.

After cleaning off the cars we arrived home safely, after having had one of the best holidays of our lives, apart from the first three days, and its several mistakes.

Rick had learned a lot that week by watching Keith English and the other artists in St Ives, and he put that knowledge into practice on his own paintings. They improved so much that he put his pictures up by 50p each!

We had enjoyed our holiday so much that we had many more (alcohol free) holidays there. St Ives is a truly beautiful place.

Back at the office on Monday morning and feeling really refreshed after our break was a bit of a blow, we were back to the usual stuff. Job after job had come in over the weekend, the usual things – house and office burglaries, thefts of scrap metal and also thefts of more pushbikes from several parts of our division.

Before I went away I'd had a tip-off from one of the local likely lads who'd had a fall out with a fellow likely lad ('Mr Bike Thief'). He'd given me the nod that Mr Bike Thief had been nicking pushbikes over the last few weeks and hiding them in a garage, so I'd circulated his name as 'wanted for questioning', but he couldn't be found. I asked around if anyone had seen him and, oddly enough, my partner John

Longbottom had seen him coming out of the dole office on the Friday that we were away not knowing that he was wanted. After going out on enquiries with John on different jobs, I decided to nip into the dole office to find out if and when my suspect was signing on there.

As I was waiting to be seen, a sheet of paper on a notice board in the internal office and away from the public, caught my eye, and after reading it I couldn't stop laughing.

At that point I was told that John was correct, and my suspect was signing on the dole there on Friday afternoon, so I thanked them very much and I also asked them for a copy of the notice, which I've saved for years. See if it makes you laugh as well.

The following sentences have been taken from actual letters received by the Social Security Department in Sheffield:

1. I am writing to the Social to say that my baby was born two years old. When do I get my money?
2. I am forwarding my marriage certificate and six children. I have seven, but one died and was baptized on one sheet of paper.
3. Mrs Cartwright has not had any clothes for a year and has been visited by the vicar regularly.
4. I cannot get sick pay. I have six children; can you tell me why?
5. I am glad to report that my husband who was reported missing, is dead.
6. This is my eighth child. What are you going to do about it?
7. Please find out for certain if my husband is dead. The man I am living with can't eat and do anything until he finds out.
8. I am very annoyed to find that you have branded my son illiterate, as this is a lie. I was married to his father a week before he was born.
9. In answer to your letter, I have given birth to twins in the enclosed envelope.

10. In accordance with your instructions, I have given birth to a boy weighing 10lbs. I hope this is satisfactory.

11. I am forwarding my marriage certificate and my three children, one of which was a mistake as you will see.

12. My husband got his project cut off two weeks ago and I haven't had any relief since.

13. Unless I get my husband's money soon, I will be forced to live an immortal life.

14. You have changed my little boy to a little girl. Will that make a difference?

15. I haven't any children as yet as my husband is a bus driver and works day and night.

16. I want money as quickly as I can get it. I have been in bed with the doctor for two weeks and he doesn't do me any good. If things don't improve I'll have to send for another doctor.

Come Friday afternoon Mr Bike Thief got the shock of his life as I'd waited around the corner until he'd signed on the dole and I told him that he was under arrest for the theft of pushbikes. He denied all knowledge of it, but when John and I took him home to search his property, there were several bikes in his sitting room and a few minutes later we found about seven or eight in his shed – we'd obviously got our man. When he knew the game was up he took us to a garage on the Manor Estate where we recovered about twenty more bikes. He hadn't sold any but was waiting to get about forty or fifty together and then he was going to sell them all at once to someone in another town. I could see that he was telling the truth.

A week or two later he arrived at court wearing a smart suit and a tie. There was an angelic look on his face and the magistrates felt sorry for him. He explained that he'd had a bad upbringing and he was given a three-month prison sentence suspended for a year, which meant that, if he kept his nose clean and kept out of trouble he would get away scot free.

Now you can see why our job was so frustrating. The time spent on the detection of the crime, along with all the paperwork required for court, had taken hours and hours. Let's face it, he was a calculated thief, making a living through stealing. I couldn't stop thinking that if he'd nicked the magistrate's bike then the punishment meted out may have been more severe.

When we came out of court he was laughing and couldn't believe that he'd got his freedom. We knew he'd be at it again and it would only be a matter of time before we caught up with him once more. A further waste of time for us was having to trace the owners of all the stolen bikes and to ensure their return to their rightful owners. What a farce, thanks Mr Magistrate.

CHAPTER 10

Gaffers, Bacon 'Sarnies' and Special Fried Rice

'**L**ook mummy – it's PC Johnson. Have you got any sweets I can give him please?'

As I turned to look at the voice I got a surprise – it was little Sally and her mum Hazel who had always been the first to arrive at school in the past. (Chapter 4, *What's Tha Up To?*). In the two years since I had last seen her she had grown and was still the first child to arrive at the school-crossing point waiting for me to take her across the dual carriageway of the busy A57 Handsworth Road. After that I knew that she would then skip her way to St Joseph's School about a hundred yards away.

I was on cloud nine and just couldn't believe that a young girl had remembered me after about two years. It was the same with some of the other kids who came to be taken across the road in a rush to get to school on time. If I heard 'PC Johnson' shouted once I must have heard it a dozen times and after I had crossed them to the other side of the dual carriageway, some were turning around to wave back at me with smiles on their faces – just the same as mine as I waved back to them.

As I crossed back over the road I had a lump in my throat and felt tears of happiness welling up in my eyes.

'Kettle's on Martyn, an't bacon's sizzling away – come on – hurry up!' It was Dennis and his mate at Oliver's butcher's shop, one of my old cup of tea spots.

'Kids have obviously missed you, looking at their little faces,' he said laughingly, 'and if you're back in uniform for good I'd best order more bacon and sausages for thi breakfast. Come on in, glad to see you back again.' With that he slapped me on the back with one hand and poured scalding hot water from the kettle into the big brown teapot with the other, as I licked my lips in anticipation of what I knew would be a cracking bacon sandwich.

A couple of weeks prior to this the Detective Chief Inspector had called me into his office for a chat. What's up now I thought, as this would be the second occasion in the last month. He was jovial enough and complimented me on some of the crimes that our team had cleared up. He was also pleased with the network of informants that I'd developed over the years, which had helped, not only our force's detection rate but also others, including the capture of Mr Spineless Bastard.

'Why haven't you taken your sergeant's exam, Johnson?' was his first question.

'Sir, with respect, I've no interest whatsoever in becoming a sergeant, it's just not my scene at all.'

He shrugged his shoulders in a resigned sort of manner just like the last time that he'd asked me the same question.

'Answer me this then, Johnson,' he said as he looked me in the eye, 'be totally honest with me. Would you rather be a detective or on the beat?'

The last time I'd seen him he'd asked me the same question and I'd dithered a bit with my answer but now having had time to think about it since then, my answer to him was prompt and I looked him in the eye.

'Without doubt, sir, not only do I prefer the beat, but that is also the place where I feel that I am more effective and doing more good. I joined the Force to work within a community and also to encourage that same community to work with me. By working with people, sir, I feel that you can get the best out of them and that is why I am happiest on the beat, working with people and not against them. Working against criminals is another matter, and as you have seen from my record I have had more than my fair share of putting them away. The other thing I feel strongly about, sir, is that if you work together with people and amongst people a lot of crime can be prevented, which in turn saves time on that crime's detection.'

As I looked at him he was slowly nodding his head in approval.

'Well done and thank you for your honest answer. You have just solved a problem for me.'

'What's that, sir?'

'We were looking to promote someone to Detective Sergeant and you haven't passed your exams. I had a good idea what your reply would be and, accordingly, I've recommended you for a new position and I think it will suit you.'

'What's that, sir?' I asked with a quizzical look on my face.

'The Chief Constable has decided that we ought to have fully experienced people working in their own community as Area Policemen, where they will be an effective tool in both preventing and detecting crime. It's a newly created post and you can choose to work your own shifts in order to make you more productive, and if you ever want the use of a police car, one will be made available. New policemen need to work with experienced policemen and I hope you will assist in doing just that, we will also need to get you back into plain clothes from time to time for any large enquiries such as a murder or something similar.

You'll be back on your old stomping ground and covering several beats, starting from Attercliffe Road right across to Darnall, Handsworth and part of the Manor Estate. You can start in a couple of weeks' time.'

My mouth had dropped open and I couldn't believe what he was saying, and he shook my hand, wished me good luck and that was it.

Walking outside the police headquarters in the city I lit a fag. I was gobsmacked and couldn't believe what he'd said. The expression 'dreams come true' came to mind. I was that excited I remember that I punched the air, forgetting that I had a cigarette in my hand, and burnt the end of my bloody nose.

Most people would love to be a detective, I know. Some people see it as being glamorous and exciting, which at times it certainly is. It's a great feeling to arrest a prolific burglar, robber or car thief and see them being sent away on 'holiday' to prison for a few months. Having been good little boys in prison, they get remission and are sent home early, laughing their heads off and ready to start all over again. Some of their mates hear how easy it was for 'Mr Burglar' to do his porridge, so they also decide to give it a go – why not? They've not much to lose and so it goes on, spiralling out of control and wasting more police time and typing paper.

I've said it before and I'll say it again, the answer is prevention and education and trying to keep the youngsters away from getting into crime in the first place.

When I joined the Force as a 19-year-old 'sprog' (novice) in 1962, the whole of our heavily populated and large police division was policed by bobbies on the beat. There was only one vehicle, a Hillman Husky Shooting Brake-type, of car containing a police driver and a police observer to cover the entire division. To drive that vehicle, you would have to be an old timer and to be an observer you had to have at least four years' experience on the beat. We also had two Aerial Leader 250cc motor cycles, if you could call them that – and that was all.

There were no mobile phones, no radios and only a 15-inch piece of wood, or truncheon, to protect ourselves with. I am proud to say that in all my fourteen years on the beat in the tough Attercliffe Division, I never hit anyone with it. Self-taught communication skills and sometimes laughter and banter, usually diffused a situation and the arrest was made. On some occasions, such as a pub fight or when facing someone with a knife, it could get really nasty and you needed to be able to handle yourself and use your fists.

As an ex-blacksmith, there was more fat on a cold chip than there was on me and at 6ft 1in and weighing in at 16½ stone I didn't lose many fights. I've never believed in gratuitous violence or bullying, but if it's necessary to use your fists, you have no option but to use them.

People have always been important to me, good or bad, black or white, young or old, rich or poor, Christian or otherwise – I respect them all unless they prove otherwise. My mum used to say that you only learn when you're listening and not when you're talking, and she was right. I used to stop and talk and listen to as many people as possible. As bobbies we were part of their community and because we'd stopped to listen to them it was amazing, at times, what they would tell you. We also respected each other, knew where to find each other if needs be and by far the vast majority of people trusted and appreciated us living amongst them. People felt safe in their beds at night and, without a doubt, because of our visible presence we prevented lots of crime.

Unfortunately, came the birth of the Panda car and the loss of the personal touch. We were driving past the older people who wanted to tell us something or the smiling school children who brought us sweets to school.

It's always been a bone of contention of mine that my seven grandchildren, some of whom are teenagers now have never ever met a policeman. What a shocking disgrace. How many kids are out there who would love to talk, in secret, to a policeman or policewoman about their problems. Problems like bullying, parental and sexual abuse or being coerced into either taking or dealing with the blight of the earth – drugs.

The regular policemen are now not there for the very people who need them, what a sad loss for society. Back in my day crimes such as murder were very rare, now they are commonplace. We are inundated on a weekly basis with statistics showing how crime is on the increase at a frightening rate. The one statistic that I have never seen shown is how much crime a good beat bobby could prevent by his very presence.

'If something is working, why mend it' comes to mind. The decision makers of today have never worked on a police beat and certainly don't appreciate its importance. Yes, I know that the world has changed but the fundamentals of life have not.

Give our kids a fighting chance of survival, open up communications and put good, regular bobbies back on the streets. Try it – I, like many other old bobbies in either city or rural areas can bear witness to the fact that it works. It has been mooted that people from industry or commerce are going to enter the police force at a high level such as superintendents. Are they going to run it like a business? What a load of tripe. The police force is not a business, it is a service to the public. There used to be an expression, certainly in our force when dealing with a new recruit, 'get your numbers dry (collar numbers – in other words you're still wet behind the ears) and really learn what the job is all about before you even think about being a gaffer', and it's true. How can you teach someone how to do the job if you haven't done it yourself?

My apologies for digressing but I think by now you will have realized how strongly I feel and how proud I am to have been a beat bobby.

Over the next few chapters you and I will be working together on the beat, we have no idea what we are going to be met with or the decisions that will have to be made – always expect the unexpected because you never ever know what's going to happen next. If you're up for it, read on ...

So, let's get back to that bacon sandwich in the butcher's shop.

The crispy bacon sarnie, larruped with brown HP sauce, followed by a pint pot of tea and a fag, made one of the happiest days of my life even better still. What more could I wish for – nothing. Dennis filled me in with the latest news, whilst at the same time ogling the young mothers as they crossed the road on their way back from dropping their kids off at school.

As I left the shop, and after licking my greasy lips I started to whistle away to myself. I was so happy to be back on the beat once more and mixing with people. I'd had a laugh with the kids earlier. We'd recently been equipped with radios and if you wanted to make a call you pressed a button and out shot an aerial about 5 inches long with a white button-shaped object at the end of it. When I was taking the kids across the road, I'd press it and pretend that I'd got the aerial stuck up my nose. They loved it, and even today and now parents themselves, if I happen to bump into them they'll remind me.

The rest of that day, I spent talking to different people on my area and explaining to them why I was there on a permanent basis. Different people had different questions which I thought was good, and a few days later I arranged to set up a regular surgery at the Darnall Church School on Station Road. Anyone wanting to discuss anything with me could do so. I was as happy as a 'pig in muck' as I was driving back up the M1 to Thorpe Hesley and home.

After tea with Christine and the kids, I decided a pint was in order to celebrate the day and so I nipped into the Mason's Arms. Friday evenings were always busy, and I could see that my mates were already in the Tap Room waiting for someone to make a four up for a game of crib. I was in like a shot and ordered a pint for myself and for the three old codgers, Harry, Les and my crib partner Wilf. Two pints later, along with lots of banter, Wilf and I were winning for a change.

Suddenly the door opened with a bang and Mr Tsang from the Chinese takeaway dashed into the room in a blind panic.

'Martyn, you come, you come,' and I thought he said something like 'counter' in broken English and he grabbed my arm.

Ming Tsang was my neighbour and was a great guy, but he and his wife spoke only an odd word of English. It must be something really serious, I thought, I'd never seen him in such a state and we both ran from the pub. My mind was racing as we entered the spotless kitchen where Mrs Tsang was in tears, whilst at the same time trying to juggle several woks on the large gas cooker. Ming then dragged me into the shop itself so that I was now behind the counter, in front of which I could see four people obviously waiting for their food. What the hell is happening here, I thought, as Ming shoved a menu into my hand and I could see that he was nearly crying, as he said, 'Martyn, you – order,' and he pointed to the menu on the counter, 'Michael Manchester. Car no go, no come home,' and he ran back into the kitchen to help Mrs Tsang cook. I was speechless and couldn't believe the crazy situation that I now found myself in. Ming and his wife couldn't speak English, and my only Chinese was to ask for 'special fried rice please'. I turned to the customers, three of whom I knew, and apologised for their obvious predicament, and I'll not tell you how many swear words I muttered under my breath.

Michael Tsang, their son, spoke perfect English and was a lovely lad. He lived with his mum and dad and every night he worked behind the counter taking orders, but tonight it sounded as if he had broken down in Manchester and wasn't going to get home before the shop closed. In Mr Tsang's panic he'd asked Christine to help behind the counter and take food orders, but she couldn't because of looking after the kids so she had sent him to look for me in the pub.

Just then the shop doorbell rang and Pete Jaques and his wife June from the village came in, wanting a large order. As soon as Pete saw me he went into hysterics.

'What's tha doing behind the counter? A copper serving in a Chinese takeaway – now I've seen everything.'

June ordered several dishes, so I hastily grabbed the menu and tried to find what was what. Eventually I got the order: 2 number 20, one with rice, one with chips; number 31 spring rolls and number 47 spare ribs Hong Kong style. What a bloody carry on, I thought, as I ran into the kitchen to give Ming the order. Ming then passed me a large bag with a completed order in it for one of the customers in the shop who had already ordered. He'd written on the cartons what was inside. The problem was that he'd written it in Chinese, so I hadn't a clue what it said. Back in the shop I tried to sort it out with the customer which order belonged to whom.

All the customers were laughing, that is until I handed them the wrong orders. I was sweating like a stuck pig. Most people knew me and I was getting some right comments, which made me even more flustered.

The door opened again, and one of the first customers that I'd served had brought their meal back, I'd given them the wrong bag of food, so I knew that someone else would be back with their wrong bag of food.

What a bloody nightmare. Sweat was dripping off my forehead and the bell went again, and another group of people came in wanting orders. Ming kept bringing food out and I kept trying to check it. Some customers were laughing at the expense of the other customers who'd taken the wrong meal home. It was like hell let loose.

By this time the people at the pub had heard that I was serving behind the counter in the takeaway and that it was total chaos; and piled into the shop to see what was happening to have a good laugh at my expense.

I could hear Mr and Mrs Tsang arguing like hell in the back kitchen. I didn't know whether I was coming or going.

Just as I thought that it couldn't get any worse, in walked Brian and Darrell Hurt, my mates from Wentworth and the biggest mickey takers of all time. They'd just come back from the races so were more than well 'oiled'. They couldn't believe their eyes when they saw me behind the counter and were bent double laughing at my predicament. They were giving it some right 'effing and geffing' and jokingly started to order 5 number 10s, 10 number 30s, etc just to wind me up. Will this nightmare ever end?

To make matters worse people were phoning in orders and I was running around like a blue-arsed fly, but I had to laugh when a few minutes later Brian, who had disappeared, came back into the shop and placed a pint of beer from the pub on the counter. He'd realized that I'd had enough and couldn't cope.

After two hours of going backwards and forwards between the shop and back kitchen it just wasn't working. There were chips here, rice there, Mrs Tsang was crying, and I realized that, although we'd tried our best, it just wasn't good enough, so we decided to shut the shop at 10pm.

I had a head like a bucket with thinking and trying to get things right and when Mr Tsang and I went outside for a fag he looked to me as if he was close to collapsing. What a night that was, an evening I'll never forget, but luckily the local people understood the Tsang's predicament and didn't make many complaints. We'd tried our best

Everybody had a good laugh, including me in the end, and they still talk about it today and that was about forty years ago. That night I went to bed and I dreamt about gaffers, bacon sarnies and fried rice.

The next day, Michael arrived back home. He'd had to travel by train and left his car to be repaired in Manchester. He was grateful that I'd helped out in the shop and thanked me profusely. He was a smashing lad and both Christine and I had a lot of respect for the whole family.

CHAPTER 11

Just Another Day at the Office!

'Help me mister, help me!' a lady shouted to me above the noise of the traffic. I'd seen her before knocking around the Darnall area, but I didn't know her name. She looked to be about 80 years of age with silver-coloured hair and she was wearing glasses, which she kept taking off and peering closely at something in her left hand. Her shopping bags were on the floor and with her right hand she was rummaging around in the pocket of her full-length apron.

It was the tea-time rush hour and, because the traffic lights at Darnall Crossroads were out of action *again*, I was working traffic control to ease the congestion. About three weeks prior to this occasion the traffic lights had broken down for the first time and for that reason I was also working the rush hour traffic. It was really busy and the noise from the volume of traffic was sometimes deafening. Suddenly, through the noise, I thought I could hear a cat purring and looked down at my feet to see a little black kitten slithering around my ankles. Where the hell has he come from and how's he got here, in the middle of the road with all this traffic racing about, how hasn't he got run over? I thought.

I could see that he was frightened, which was perfectly understandable. I couldn't pick him up and he quite simply just cowered around my feet until the traffic eased and got back to normal. How the little kitten had survived the volume of traffic and made his way to me in the middle of this wide junction I'll never know. Much to the delight of the people who had been watching I picked up the poor little thing, took off my helmet and placed him inside it, until I'd got back to the pavement. The crowd and especially the kids were all clapping. The kitten had no collar, and nobody seemed to know who it belonged to, so after borrowing a cardboard box from Wigfall's electrical shop, I took it home, much to the delight of our little son and daughter, Richard and Sally. 'Lucky' as we called him, lived happily with us for the next sixteen years.

Back to the present. I looked across at the lady, who looked quite calm and asked her to give me a few minutes and then I would get to her as quick as I could when the traffic had eased, but her reply shook me.

'Yes, that's alright love, but I need some help, I've been robbed.'

Blimey, I wasn't expecting that as she looked so calm. Robbery was another matter. After a couple of minutes, I was able to leave my post in the middle of the junction and went to the lady. By this time, she was holding her purse in one hand and a load of coins in the other. I gave a silent chuckle to myself as I thought I knew what the problem was.

Over the last few weeks I'd seen lots of different people in similar situations to the old lady, holding money with one hand and scratching their head with the other, and asking for my help.

'I see that you've been shopping today, love,' I said to her.

'Yes, I have and that's why I've shouted you, I've been robbed. Them shopkeepers have diddled me out of some money I'm sure. They've not given me the right change.'

I was right, and I could see that she was holding a handful of the new decimal coins. When the old pounds, shillings and pence system went decimal in February 1971 it caused a massive problem, especially to old people like the lady I was now talking to. Instead of old half crowns, florins, shillings, sixpences, threepenny bits, pennies and half pennies we now had fifty pence, twenty pence, ten pence, five pence, two pence, one pence and half pence coins to contend with. It wasn't just confusing to old people, it was confusing to younger people like myself and you could see people walking out of shops looking at their change and trying to decide whether they'd been robbed or otherwise. It took months for all the country to get accustomed to the new money.

I checked the lady's change for her, explained what was what, and she was quite happy once more.

'Thank you for that, young man, I get so confused as I've got older and these new-fangled coins make it more confusing still. Would you like a cup of tea, I only live around the corner?'

I was certainly up for that and gladly followed her for tea and biscuits. I used to see Mary for years afterwards and we always had a chat and a laugh or a wave from across the road – proper police work, everybody happy.

Walking up Handsworth Road from Darnall and chatting with people who I hadn't seen for ages was great and I caught up with the local gossip. As I walked further I could see that what had once been Rex Gray's gym had now closed down for some reason, and it brought back some memories.

In my first week on the job I found myself in terrible lodgings in Hall Road just behind the gym. So, not knowing a soul in Sheffield, I decided to nip into the gym and possibly join. Slipping a jacket on over my blue police shirt and tie, blue trousers and wearing black boots, in I went through the door. You could have heard a pin drop as everybody looked at me and twigged what I did for a living. I was so naive back then and I could hear whispered comments like 'copper', and 'what does he f_____ want in here?'

'Can I help you?' asked a bloke who later told me that his name was Billy Calvert, a very well-known locally born featherweight boxer.

'Do you do weight training here?' I asked nervously, and the crowd of rough looking lads seemed to relax – unlike me.

'We train boxers here, but if you want an hour with the weights, join the lads over there in that corner of the gym.' He pointed towards a group of well-muscled chaps.

As I walked across, Billy shouted and asked them to show me how to go on, and I noticed one or two sniggers coming from them. I'd done a bit of weight lifting before so one of the lads put some weights onto the bar. As I lifted it above my head and then put it down more weights were put on at either end, which obviously weren't as easy to lift, but I managed it. The look on the lads' faces was one of surprise, at last the penny dropped. I realized why they were sniggering, as they put yet more weights onto the bar. At this point people were coming to watch this young copper make a prat of himself. No way could he lift that above his head, and I thought that they were right. As I steadied myself to try and lift the heavy weights I remembered my tutor-bobby, Roy Sharman's words to me, on my very first day on the job: 'just remember, if you earn respect you will get it back'.

By this time all the lads were nudging each other and even Billy Calvert came to watch. It was either 'shit or bust' as I took the strain and started to lift. Bloody hell, I thought, they're trying to kill me. Slowly, I moved the weights upwards with a great struggle and then first one, then another was shouting, 'Come on lad, come on, you can do it, push, push, push, keep going, push, which I did and finally my arms locked in a 'clean' lift. I was well and truly knackered, it was the heaviest lift that I had ever done, and as I sat down on the bench, people were patting me on the back in congratulations. I realized that I'd passed 'their' test and the atmosphere towards me from then on was totally different – I'd thankfully earned their respect.

I used to call in on occasions when I had the opportunity and I kept in touch with some of the lads for years.

One of them was called Tommy Nolan, a proper tough character, and we got on like a house on fire. He was as tough as old boots and throughout his life illegal fighters (bare-knuckle boxers) such as gypsies, were always wanting to fight him. I thought a lot about Tommy and him about me, he was truly one of life's characters and certainly one of the hardest men that I have ever met.

Billy Calvert was a first-class boxer and in February 1963, a year after I'd first met him, he fought Scottish featherweight champion Bobby Fisher in Kelvin Hall, Glasgow. Billy was easily the underdog and it was the highlight of his career when he stopped Fisher within the distance and won the fight. After his fighting career Billy led an interesting life. He went on to own the King's Head pub in Attercliffe and never once did I have to go there because of any trouble – well done Billy and thanks for helping me out on my first week on the job. Billy sadly passed away on 10 August 2016 aged 82, a very well-respected man.

I loved working the beat – you never knew what would happen next or who you were going to meet. One sunny afternoon I was walking down Tinsley Park Road which was at the side of the canal. The canal was used a lot in those days, mainly by barges transporting iron or coal towards Attercliffe where it then continued into the heart of the city. It was a very busy waterway.

As I crossed Broughton Lane (where the canal runs under the bridge) and as I got to the other side of the road, I could see a barge and it looked as though there was nobody aboard. Just as I was about to walk past it and continue on my way to Attercliffe police station, I heard a voice shout, 'are you looking for a body?' and I turned to see a man walking up the steps from the living quarters of the barge.

'Sorry, what did you say?'

'Are you looking for a body?'

I thought I was going mad, just what was he on about?

'What do you mean, am I looking for a body, mate?'

'I've just been in contact with you lads and they said they were sending round a police car. I thought that it was you. I've just found a body and because I'm laden, the barge was near the bottom of the canal and I've got a body wrapped around the propeller.'

'Are you joking, or what?'

'No, I've got a body wrapped around the propeller, come and look.'

Just as I was walking to speak with the bargeman, a Panda car pulled up containing Harold Singleton, the sergeant, and a policeman that I'd never seen before. I realized that the guy on the barge must be right after all. They both got out of the car and Sergeant Singleton spoke: 'Martyn, glad you're here, this is a fairly new recruit called Graham Glover. He's been on the Force for a week or two but has never dealt with a dead body before. We were going to deal with the incident but now I can leave him with you, you can show him how to go on. I'll leave you with the car and I'll walk back to the Police station – okay?'

'Okay, Serge. You've just spoilt my quiet day,' I said as I shook hands with Graham. At the same time saying, 'come on lad, let's see what's what.'

The barge was pulled into the side of the tow path and the bloke was right, I could see a leg sticking up in the air. Poor Graham's face was a picture. The bargeman loaned me some gloves and then him and I both managed to disentangle the male body from the propeller and onto the bank. What a bloody mess!

'I've found one or two bodies in the canal in my life, but this one's been in some time by the looks of it,' the bargeman said.

As I looked at the crumpled body on the bank, I explained to Graham that, in my opinion, it wasn't a suicide. For some reason, when people commit suicide by drowning they usually leave a note somewhere, and something that I've always found weird, is that they take their clothes off and leave them in a pile before entering into the water – but this one was fully clothed and still had his boots on. The other interesting thing is that a body once drowned usually sinks to the bottom and over a period of a few days fills with gas, and then comes back up to the surface, but this one looks to have been down in the mud for a long time. As I looked up I could see that all I had said to Graham had gone in one ear and out of the other. His mouth had dropped open and he was as white as a sheet. He'd obviously not seen anyone dead before.

Even though the man on the barge had left his details with the office I took them again and re-examined the body – fully clothed, in a dark suit and wearing dark boots. It appeared that the man had fallen in as there was no suggestion of him being weighted down with anything and no signs of foul play.

A search of all his pockets revealed no information about him whatsoever. I told the man on the barge that it was okay for him to go and I sent for the mortuary people to come and remove the body.

I looked at Graham again and during all this he hadn't spoken a word, he looked terrified.

'Right, let's get him undressed here on the bank. It'll save us a bit of time doing it at the mortuary. You take his boots and socks off and I'll start at the top.'

As I started to remove his shirt and jacket you could see that the body had been in the water for a long, long time – he was totally decomposed. By this time Graham had taken off a boot and as he removed the sock, the flesh on the man's leg came off with the sock, which left Graham holding a sock full of soggy remains. His face got whiter. Poor lad. What a way to see your first 'stiff'.

The van arrived and took the body to the mortuary and we followed on behind.

The mortuary staff took over the body which was essentially a skeleton, and we left a report. There were no missing persons reported in Sheffield matching the man's description and photographs of clothing were sent out to different forces in the hope that he could be identified but he never was. Unfortunately, someone, somewhere was left wondering what happened to their loved one, friend, brother, son or husband.

By the time we left the mortuary, I was starving hungry, so we called for fish and chips to eat in the car. Graham didn't want to know and was still gipping at what he had seen. He was a big, good looking lad of about 6' 5" and, although he was quiet now, I was to find out over the next few years that he wasn't quiet at all.

By this time, it was dark and as we drove through Burngreave and down towards the traffic lights at Fir Vale I idly glanced at a car going in the opposite direction. For some reason, I had funny vibes about it and much to Graham's amazement I slammed the breaks on and, with blue light flashing, I turned the car round and sped off after him. As he turned right, without giving a signal, and entered the Norwood estate, he turned so fast that he nearly overturned the car, and I followed. Within a hundred yards, I'd lost him, he must have turned right into what I knew to be a cul-de-sac, and when we retraced our steps sure enough, there was the car, parked up behind a privet hedge. He could be anywhere by now, I thought, so I went to check out the vehicle.

Just as I opened the driver's door a youth of about seventeen years of age jumped out and, at the same time, head-butted me in the face. I let fly with my fist which knocked him backwards into the privet hedge where Graham grabbed and handcuffed the little pillock. Another tooth gone, lips looking like heavy-duty tyres, I was getting uglier by the day, but I resisted the urge to give him another – he'd already got a black eye on its way and a bloody nose. The keys were in the ignition and so we locked up the car and took him back to the station.

Back at the nick I left Graham to deal with the prisoner while I signed off duty and headed home to try and find an ice pack. My face was giving me some right stick.

CHAPTER 12

Attercliffe Police Box – If only it could Talk

The following morning, when Christine saw my heavy-duty lips and yet another gap in my teeth – making them look like a garden fence – she went crackers. I've never looked right pretty but I now looked pretty awful. We didn't have time to discuss it further as a knock at the door revealed, of all people, young Graham, the new bobby from the day before, along with a very attractive young lady. As the customary introductions were being made between the four of us I wondered why he was visiting. The young lady was Sally, Graham's girlfriend, and as she looked at my bruised face, I saw her wince.

As Christine was mashing us all a pot of tea I asked him about, what turned out to be, his first prisoner, 'Mr Carnicker'.

'When you left the nick last night, a detective took over the case. The lad admitted to stealing the car keys from his father's jacket pocket and then taking the car out for a spin. The detective then spoke to the owner of the car who didn't even know that it had been stolen. The owner, his father, is a doctor at the Northern General hospital and had certainly not given him permission to drive, and went ballistic at his son's stupidity. The detective then charged Mr Carnicker with the theft of the car, no driving licence, no insurance and assaulting you, Martyn. He was then bailed to appear at court at a later date and we then dropped him back at his house and gave his dad his car keys back.'

'Well done Graham, I'll give you a witness statement for you to pass on to the detective tomorrow. Well done lad!'

At that point, Sally, who appeared to be very shy, spoke up and said, 'Martyn, is it true that Graham dealt with a dead body in the canal yesterday that was messy?'

'Yes love, why?'

'I thought he must be kidding. Was he alright with it?'

Through my bruised lips I had to chuckle as, in my mind's eye, I could see Graham standing on the canal bank having removed the man's sock which was full of fleshy pulp. He'd looked ashen when he asked me, 'What shall I do with this, Martyn?' and I had said to him, 'well he won't be needing that anymore, so sling it back in the canal.' Which he did.

'I'm surprised that he didn't faint,' Sally said. 'I would have.' And I could see her shudder at the thought of it.

'He dealt with it very well, it was far too gone to smell because it had been in the water for a long time. Yes, he did okay.'

Suddenly Graham leaned forward, looked at me and said, 'Right. How?'

'What do you mean, how?' I said.

'How did you know – I'm intrigued and want to know, how?'

'Know, what?'

'Last night with that car.'

What the hell was he on about? My head was spinning, and my lips were hurting, and now I thought I was going crackers. What is he on about?

'Graham, for crying out loud, tell me what you're on about.'

'How did you know that that car was stolen? I want to learn how you knew.'

'I didn't know Graham, it was just a hunch. That's why I turned to follow him.'

'But you must have had a reason.'

'I can't tell you because I don't know myself.' That was the only answer that I could give him. 'The only way I can explain it Graham, although it's difficult, is that it's experience. You'll find out that over the years you'll probably end up doing the same. It could be the way he was driving when I first clapped eyes on him, it could be a nervous look he gave or something as simple as not looking at the police car. The only thing I can say is that if I have a hunch or a niggle I can't settle until I've done something about it. Last night we won one, we were lucky – better to try and fail than not to try at all. If I were that clever though Graham, I'd have worked out that he was going to head-butt me in the face, but I wasn't, that's why I'm getting uglier and talking like a stuffed dummy.'

Sally and Graham were a lovely couple and we became good friends. Graham was a great bloke and I could tell that he would become a good copper.

After a few days off sick and a cowardly visit to the dentist I was back on the beat again and had a message left for me to ring Dr _____ at the Northern General hospital. When I rang him back the doctor answered in a very polite voice. 'I understand that you were one of the officers who arrested my son the other night for stealing my car.'

'That's correct, sir, how can I help you?'

'I also understand that you got injured and that one of the officers retaliated. If it was you and, I don't want you to answer me if it was, I would like to apologise for my son's behaviour and stupidity. It sounds as if he got what he justly deserved and was knocked down a peg or two. He's been nothing but a pain in the arse the last couple of years and I think that this has calmed him down. Once again, I hope you're not too badly hurt and thank you.'

As I set off to walk up Attercliffe Road, or the 'Cliffe' as we call it, towards the police box at the junction with Staniforth Road I was well chuffed to think that the doctor had asked about my health and also the fact that he was pleased that we'd helped him straighten his son out. Not what I expected at all when I returned his call.

I opened the police box door with a key that fitted every police box in Sheffield and looked through the purple-coloured glass windows. I could see everyone, but no one

could see me, so I lit up a fag. In the last two years as a
detective I'd not used this police box and it brought back
some happy memories. Inside was a telephone which could
also be reached and used by the public for an emergency
from outside. There was also a plank of wood big enough
to form a desk and a chair to sit on in order for us to write
reports.

When I was first on the beat, the sergeant knew exactly
where you were meant to be because of a pre-designated
route, and every 20 minutes you had to be at a geographical
point, and on every hour, you had to be where there was a pay
phone or police box. This was to enable the sergeant to make
sure that we were alright and to pass on any information that
we may require. In the early days we had no radios and if you
had a violent prisoner you had to drag him to the nearest
police box and ring for assistance. Also, in the police box was
a book containing details and pictures of known criminals,
which allowed us to remember the pictures and recognise
them if we saw them on the street.

In 1962/3 the winter snow was extremely heavy all over
the country. Attercliffe, because of the many steelworks,
furnaces and allied industries pumping out hot air into the
atmosphere, rarely had snow, but on this occasion it did. I
was patrolling there on night-shift, 11pm to 7am, and as I got
to the police box the phone rang. On answering it I spoke to
PC Albert Hathaway, an old timer who worked in the office.

'Martyn, you're covering Attercliffe Road as far as Washford
Bridge, aren't you?'

'Yes.'

'A taxi driver's phoned the office to say that he's seen quite
a few rats in the Washford Bridge area. I laughingly told him
that this was nothing new and left it at that. But I thought I'd
let you know just for information, that's all.'

I had to check that all the shops were secure by trying the
handles on the front and back doors and ensure that the
windows were intact. We all had to do this once before our

meal and once after our meal. As I got to the junction with Effingham Road I started to hear squeaking noises.

What the hell's that I thought, but then I realized that it was getting louder and louder still. The old police torches weren't very good in those days and suddenly the noise grew even louder, and I could hear the scratchings of scampering feet. What the bloody hell is going off? Luckily, I was near to one of the gas lamps and boy was I glad for that, as I could see coming towards me across the whole width of the road thousands and thousands of rats. I couldn't believe my eyes and even Tarzan couldn't have shinned up that gas lamp and up to the cross bar as quickly as I did. Wave, after wave of them went past heading in the general direction of Rotherham. I'd never seen anything like it and, after the rats had gone I went to the nearest phone box at the corner of Effingham Street and phoned Albert, who thought I was kidding him.

I made my way back to the police box, scratching my head in total disbelief at what I had seen. When I got back to the main nick at Attercliffe for my snap another bobby had witnessed the same scenario down by Weedon Street and he'd just managed to jump into a phone box in time. I've never seen anything like it before or since, but we were later told by some expert on these matters from the Cleansing Department that this mass migration had occurred twice in the last 25 years, the last one being near to Hillsborough when the River Don burst its banks. It had been witnessed before when London was blitzed and also, some years previous to this, when Sheffield got bombed in the war.

It was certainly a sight I'll never forget.

Attercliffe Road was always busy, and the diversity of shops meant that people came from far and wide to do their weekly shopping. In some respects, although only a suburb of the city, it was more like a little city within a city. By far the biggest building down the Cliffe was the massive John Banners departmental store where you could buy almost anything. It used to be nicknamed the Harrods of the North and it housed only the second moving stairway outside of London.

On this particular occasion I had been in the police box for some twenty minutes, writing a report by hand and I gave myself a fag break whilst idly watching the people and vehicles going past. I was looking across at the notorious Dog and Partridge pub when I noticed that people had stopped walking and were pointing up in the air, first one and then another. What the hell's going off I thought. Fag stubbed out and helmet on, I dashed outside, and it appeared that they were all pointing in the direction of Banners. I could also see people running about on the pavement, and they were also looking straight up in the air. At the very top of this massive building, and very high up at roof level I could see a gantry-type structure hanging down from the roof. Instead of the wooden platform being level, it was now pointing towards the floor and it appeared that one of the steel cables holding it up must have broken off and there, dangling from the other cable holding the wooden board was a chap of about 40, with his legs kicking and hanging on by both of his hands for dear life. As I raced towards the scene I could see that a small crowd had gathered at the scene. What the hell do you do first? (just remember you're working the beat with me, what would you do?) The last thing to do is panic.

The poor man was yelling his head off and if he'd have fallen at that moment, he'd not only have killed himself after a fall of approximately 80ft but also people on the pavement below him. So, I hastily moved the crowd to one side and ascertained that someone had telephoned the fire brigade, as the poor man was desperately, desperately trying to hang on.

I yelled up to tell him that the fire brigade was on its way with a turntable ladder and to hang on. At one point he was hanging on by one hand and then he would swap back and use the other. The lack of blood in his arms must have been making them really painful, and although frightening, he probably did the right thing by lowering one arm to get the blood back and then by changing hands he managed to keep hanging on. The tension was amazing, and we were all willing him on. At one point I grabbed a fag and then realized that, because I was in full uniform I couldn't smoke it.

A minute seemed like an hour and we all knew that he could fall at any second. Probably a minute later and just when it looked as though he couldn't hold on any longer, the fire brigade arrived. The ladder went up and much to everybody's relief the man was brought down to safety and everyone, including me, clapped the man's bravery.

It was nerve jangling for us never mind the poor man hanging on for dear life. Once down on the ground I handed him a fag, but he was shaking so much he couldn't light it, so I lit it for him.

Someone from Banners brought him a cup of strong tea with plenty of sugar in it and unbelievably he refused it saying, 'I haven't got time for cups of tea, I've got to mend that gantry and finish the job, or my boss will go crackers.'

Fifteen minutes later he was back on the job. I couldn't decide whether he was mad or very, very brave.

The next incident that I recalled was one that I'll never forget, let's see what you think. During the same winter of '62/63 I was on night shift and writing a report in the police box. There was no one else knocking about because of the snow and you could have heard a pin drop. As I glanced through the window at about 1am I could see, on the other side of the road, two lads of about 25, one bigger than the other and pushing an empty sack barrow through the snow. They were looking around furtively and then they turned down by the side of the Dog and Partridge and into Oaks Green.

Sheffield was the steel capital of the world in those days and scrap was being stolen all the time. Although I didn't know them I could see that they were 'likely lads' and were most probably up to no good, so I tiptoed out and followed their tracks in the snow. Almost at the bottom of Oaks Green was a row of empty houses which were due to be demolished for some reason or other. As I got to an entry between them the tracks had stopped, and it was quite apparent to me that they were going to be stealing scrap metal from within the houses themselves, and also the outside toilets. After taking off my helmet I peeped around the corner and up the passage way. Framed in the light from a nearby works I could see, at the top of the entry, the larger of the two lads who was, presumably, the 'lookout man'.

A couple of minutes later I could hear banging coming from one of the outside toilets of the yard of the empty houses. Bingo! They were obviously in the act of stealing lead piping and copper ballcocks from the toilet cistern. The lad at the top of the passage, looked to be a big lad so I drew my truncheon in readiness. Our instructions when using a truncheon were to hit them either on the collarbone, elbow, wrist or knee in order to disable them, but there was also another use which I was about to deploy.

As I slowly crept up the passageway, and nearer to the big fellow who had his back to me, I held the truncheon, not by the handle but in the middle of it. I had to get it right. My intention was to grab the back of his collar with my left hand and with my right hand holding the truncheon, I would shove it between his legs, and then turn my wrist so that the truncheon was in a horizontal position. By raising my right arm, it would connect with his knackers which meant that he couldn't get away from me! Because of all the banging he didn't hear me coming and within a split second I had him, back of the collar with my left hand and truncheon through the legs. I twisted the truncheon to the horizontal position and at the same time I raised my arm quickly. He was now on his tiptoes and going nowhere.

All this had happened in a split second when suddenly the man I was holding shouted at the top of his voice to his mate, who was chopping away at the scrap metal in the outside toilet, 'It's f-----g copper!'

At this point the hammering stopped and the voice from the toilet shouted back, 'it's not f-----g copper, you thick bastard, it's LEAD!'

I was almost hysterical with laughing and the big man was struggling to get away, so I raised my right hand a bit more which slowed him down and by now he was on his tiptoes trying to avoid the pain, and with a very *squeaky* voice shouted, 'No I mean it's a proper copper, run!'

At last the lad in the outside toilet had got the message and ran out of the toilet, jumped over a wall and I never saw him again. Even though I'd got the prisoner, I just couldn't help but laugh out loud. What a comical farce.

The big man realized the game was up and I somehow managed to drag him, in spite of his sore knackers, back to the police box where I called for a car to take us back to the station.

It has to rank as one of the funniest arrests that I ever made and even now, 55 years after the event, I still laugh out loud when I think about it. 'Mr Knackerman' wouldn't grass his mate up and wasn't in possession of any stolen metal, so instead of going to court and faffing about with all the paperwork, I decided to give him a caution instead.

I hope you're enjoying your time on the beat – I told you to be ready for anything.

CHAPTER 13

My Youngest Ever Prisoner?

'**B**limey, you look smart today, Martyn – you look like a brand-new recruit on his first day as a policeman,' said Sarah.

'It's a special day today, Sarah. It's the annual Darnall Medical Aid Parade and with me being the Darnall area bobby, I've been invited to lead the parade.'

Over the past couple of days, I'd been 'bulling' up my best parade boots and they were so shiny that you could see your face in them – not a pretty sight I know. A new shirt with its separate starched collar, trousers with creases in them that sharp you could shave with them, white gloves and I was ready for off.

After kissing Christine and the kids, Richard and Sally, cheerio I drove down the recently opened M1 to work and I was furious with myself, as it was then that I realized I'd forgotten my snap box, so I called into Sarah's café for a pot of tea and a sarnie before going to the parade.

It being Easter Monday I was surprised to see the café open, but as Sarah said, she lived on the premises, so why not? Sarah was a really nice, kind-hearted person who I needed to speak to anyway. Her partner Sam, was a great guy, but over the past few months he had changed. Sam and his brother were both Asian and both owned cafés. His brother, though, was unlike Sam and I knew him to be a nasty piece of work. Sam was frightened of his brother and had been coerced into doing some driving for him. According to Sarah, who was worried sick, he drove to Dover on a fairly regular basis in a large transit van with an extended roof space. In his sleep she'd heard Sam talk about drugs and smuggling people into the country.

As I'd walked through the café and into the kitchen I'd noticed old Cyril, who was the most educated, down-and-out tramp that I ever knew. He didn't smell and wasn't particularly dirty even though he lived in parks and slept on park benches. In the early summer months, you could sometimes see him having a strip-wash in the stream in the woods at the back of Pipworth Road before anybody got up for work. His mum and dad had both died in quick succession which had sent him a bit odd. He couldn't stand the loneliness of the house, so he sold it and just wandered around the Attercliffe area with a large shopping trolley containing newspapers which he would wrap around himself to keep warm in winter.

Cyril was very well-educated and could tell you almost everything you wanted to know, he was like a modern-day Google.

'I'm having a bacon and egg sandwich, Cyril, do you want one?' I asked.

'Yes please, that's very, very kind of you, and could I have another cup of tea please?' Cyril answered very politely.

When the café was quiet like it was then, Sarah would allow him in and provide him with a free cup of tea, and we both knew what would happen with the tea when he got it. My own dad used to have four teaspoons full of sugar in his tea, but Cyril used to have TWELVE, much to Sarah's dismay. He ate when he could, usually from people's generosity but he used to say that sugar kept up his energy levels.

I paid for our sandwiches and having given Cyril his, he wolfed it down in no time, and it was obvious that he hadn't eaten for quite a while, so I was glad I'd bumped into him.

I went back into the kitchen to talk to Sarah and she told me that several weeks after my last visit Sam had been sent on another job by his brother, but he was very reluctant to go, and she had no idea where he was sent to. After that she didn't see him for over two weeks, and having asked his brother where he was, she was getting nowhere and so reported him missing.

I asked her whether she had heard anything about Sam after she had reported him missing and she replied, 'Not a thing, Martyn,' and she burst into tears. She then continued, 'I can't sleep and I'm worried sick. That's why I've opened today, it just helps to take my mind off things.'

After Sam had gone missing I'd reported what Sarah had told me about the drugs and people smuggling to the head of CID, and I was later told that the vehicle had been stopped on its way back from Dover and all it contained was 'one-armed bandit' machines. I didn't believe for one minute that it had been stopped and checked and neither did Sarah. Sam was never traced and later Sarah sold the business and moved on.

I left the café and as I started to walk further up Darnall Main Road, I was amazed to see how many old-fashioned and spotlessly clean lorries there were parked up alongside the long routeway. There were loads of them and all had been decked out with floral decorations depicting different scenes. Parents had gone to the trouble of dressing up their sons and daughters and were putting them on the lorries ready for setting off on the parade. Members of the Constance Grant Dancing School from Handsworth were on one of the floats as was the Darnall Medical Aid Queen and her attendants. It was great to know that so many local firms and businesses had mucked in by both sponsorship and loan of vehicles to make the parade a success as well as helping to raise money for the charity.

Although I hadn't seen it before, the parade had been started on an annual basis, some five or six years earlier and attracted people and businesses not only from Sheffield but also from much further afield.

As its name implies, Darnall Medical Aid was started to raise money for medical treatments of the poor and elderly people in times of need, until the birth of the National Health Service in 1948.

Lots of different organizations took part including the brownies and guides, cubs and scouts and nurses. Various steel works dressed up their lorries, as did coal suppliers and loads of others, too numerous to mention. There were marching bands and even a jazz band was on one of the lorries. People were milling around in their hundreds and organizing everyone to their places ready for the start of the parade.

As I walked past the first lorry in the procession I was trying to get my mind ready for the correct route, taking into consideration the crowds. For safety reasons there were also police officers walking at the sides and also one at the rear of the procession.

As I got to the front and put my white gloves on, suddenly, I thought I could hear, 'ONE, TWO, THREE CID IN UNIFORM'. Oh no, I thought, surely not – and as I turned around to look, there on the first float were men dressed as women and I could see, of all people, blowing kisses at me, George with his long blonde wig on. George was also accompanied by two other 'queens', Barry and Derek (or Soft Cock as people used to call him), three of the guys – sorry girls, no sorry lads (I didn't know what to call them in the end) from Mucky Mary's pub. I could hear Derek saying to Barry in an effeminate voice, 'doesn't he look smart. I've never seen him in a uniform before. Ooh I'd love to see his truncheon!' and they all giggled. All the people who went into Mucky Mary's were great characters in their own right. What a mixed bunch they were. I didn't have time to speak to them as we were ready for off.

At either side of the front of the lorry I saw two male fairies in their tutus and wigs – what a comical pair they looked. I knew the one on the left was Ernest Morley aka the Queen of Darnall. He was an ex-miner and then later a male nurse at Weston Park hospital, where he'd seen some nasty things. These experiences had prompted him and his mate, the other fairy, to raise thousands of pounds for cancer research over the years – they both deserved medals.

'Is everybody ready?' I shouted. 'One, two, three, go!'

The jazz band started, and we were off. We went up Main Road, left onto Staniforth Road and straight through the major road junction with Prince of Wales Road where other policemen had already stopped the traffic for us. The bands were playing, the crowds were in their thousands and everyone was happy. The money tins were rattled at the people watching and they all gave generously by putting money into the collecting tins. The atmosphere was fantastic.

A minute later I turned the parade left into Waverley Rd and then almost immediately right into Elmham Road and as I got to my old lodgings at number 58, Mrs Proctor, my old landlady and her family had all turned out to watch. The whole of Elmham Road was lined with people all having a lovely time and waving not just at the fairies but to everyone who passed in the parade. I, for one, was thoroughly enjoying myself and proud to be part of it.

You could hear the money boxes being rattled and filling up nicely. Well done to everybody, I thought.

The last left-hand turn was coming up and once we were on Logan Road we'd walk a short distance down the hill and we would soon enter High Hazels Park. Just before the gates to the park on the left was Gough's shop and I knew that there would be dozens of kids queuing up for their ice lollies, pop and sarsaparilla. Then not far up the hill to the bandstand where the parade would stop, and my job would be over. Then I could enjoy mixing and talking to the hundreds of people in the crowds.

Just as I got near to the end of Elmham Road and was about to turn the procession into Logan Road, I saw a flash of movement from my right and a child shot out of the crowd and ran the short distance towards me. What the hell's going on now, I thought, as I wondered why the youngster's parents weren't looking after him. The parade and its lorries were still moving forward so I quickly scooped the little child into my arms and only then did I realize that it was my own three-year-old son Richard. I couldn't believe it. He was in no danger whatsoever because I was several yards in front of the floats and as he flung his arms around my neck I was desperately looking for Christine in the crowd to pass him back to her. The problem was that I was still moving forward and Christine, I found out later, was desperately trying to get out of the crowd to get young Richard back.

I felt a right twerp but had no option than to keep walking onto Logan Road and then into the park still carrying little Richard who'd got his arms tightly round my neck. Hundreds of people watching the parade saw my predicament and people were clapping, not knowing that it was my own son that I was carrying.

As we climbed the steep hill to the top of the park, I could feel sweat running down my face and I was more than glad when I halted the parade. At this point Christine, who was also sweating after having run up the hill with Sally in a pushchair arrived and was most upset and full of apologies.

'I'm ever so sorry, I heard Richard shout 'daddy'; he'd obviously seen you and he wriggled away from me and just ran up to you.'

'Don't worry, there was never any danger because there was no traffic and looking at the laughing faces of the crowds, I think they enjoyed the situation. Come on let's find a pot of tea at the café.'

After finding the café, Christine fed Sally and Richard and I sneaked around a corner for a well-earned fag after which we then mixed with the crowd of hundreds. I bumped into my mate, Mr Dar, who was a tailor. After having learned his trade in Pakistan he'd moved to England with his family several years before. He'd asked me if I could help his children to read and write in English, and as I was single back then with plenty of time on my hands, I gladly agreed. They were great people and were very pleased to see us just as much as we were pleased to see them.

Christine's mum was there along with her sister Barbara and brother-in-law Brian together with their children Bramwell and Kelvin.

It was a wonderful afternoon and in aid of a very worthy cause. I put three quid into Ernest's collecting tin who was as high as a kite and very excited and just like the year before, he'd been selected as the best-dressed fairy queen. Prizes were dished out for the best float, best fancy dress, and so on. It was such a happy occasion and there was no trouble anywhere. It was lovely to see mums and dads with their picnics, sitting on the grass. There were games and rides for the kids, a crazy golf course and, of course, the boating lake to keep everyone entertained.

I'm not sure who announced it, but much to my embarrassment, and amongst the thanks coming from the loudspeaker system, a man said, 'I think we'd all like to thank our new regular local policemen PC Johnson who managed to keep the parade moving forward, even though part way, enroute to the park he had to rescue a lost little boy – possibly his youngest ever prisoner.' He laughingly went on to say, 'we've only just found out that, that same little boy was in fact his own son.' Everybody cheered and clapped, and I felt a right berk. 'For anyone who hasn't met PC Johnson, he's a Barnsley man and very amenable unless you've done something wrong. He and his family are knocking about somewhere in the crowd, don't be frightened to talk to him, he'll not bite. Thank you to his family for being here with us today.'

Although occasions like these were done in order to raise money for worthwhile charities, it being Easter when most people were off from their daily grind, the man was right, and it was a perfect opportunity for me to meet people I didn't know and equally as important for them to get to know me.

For the rest of the afternoon we mingled with lots and lots of different families, some of whom I knew already but others I had never met before. It truly was a fabulous afternoon and more than worthwhile for public relations.

Gough's shop at the bottom of Logan Road and next to the entrance of High Hazels Park, was really busy and doing a roaring trade. Easter Monday was the only day that they made candy floss, and lots of kids could be seen with pink sugar round their mouths, including our son Richard. Sally was covered in ice cream as it had melted on her chin and run down onto her dress and Christine was hoping that the two balloons she was holding would make it home without getting either blown away or burst.

By the time it was all over all of us were ready for home.

When we got back I was turning into our drive and I saw Mr Tsang from the Chinese takeaway next door, standing in the doorway to his shop. Bloody hell, I thought, don't tell me that Michael's missing again and I've got to take orders in the takeaway tonight, what a nightmare that would be. As he stepped aside I could see Michael behind him. What a relief. In any case I'd just remembered that they didn't open on Monday anyway and they were just about to go out for the evening. Probably to the casino in Sheffield.

After we got the kids bathed and into bed I went around to the Mason's Arms for a quick pint and a game of crib. What a great day that was!

CHAPTER 14

25th October 1973

To say it was the 25th October and winter would soon be on its way, it was quite a bit warmer than what you'd expect at that time of year and I was looking forward to what the day would throw at us.

My last pot of tea had been at about 8am and I was ready for another. The Woodburn Road School lollipop lady was off ill and so I decided to put myself on 8am to 4pm shift so that I could cover the school crossing for her. For that reason, and because I had to drop some paperwork off in the city, I decided to borrow a Panda car for the day instead of walking the beat. Little was I to know then what a good decision it was to borrow the vehicle.

I picked up the car at about 7.50am and decided to have my breakfast at Audrey and Rene's café at the junction with Woodburn Road and Worthing Road, and right next to the school – perfect. Because I'd been in the CID for a couple of years I didn't get in to see Audrey and Rene as much as I used to, and I was looking forward to seeing them again.

Up the two recently scoured steps I went, and the back door was wide open as if I was expected. Rene was in the kitchen and, as usual, she was dashing from one piece of equipment to another. Audrey was taking food orders in the front of the café. I could see that both girls were working flat out trying to get the food to the workmen as quickly as possible in order that they could get back to their jobs on time.

Grabbing an armful of cut loaves, I went to the toasting machine in the corner of the kitchen. It would only take four slices at a time and when they were done I buttered them and passed them to Rene. Fifteen minutes later the main rush was over, and Audrey passed me a mug of tea. I didn't have to ask for a sarnie, as Rene had remembered and passed me a bacon, egg and proper tomato sandwich, which I wolfed down in minutes – time to get those kids across the road to school.

'Nice to see you back, Martyn and thanks for your usual help with the toast,' Rene said. I'd earned my keep and said my cheerio's after first picking up the bread wrappers from six loaves and putting them in the bin.

I didn't know the kids at Woodburn Road School as it was just out of my area, but it turned out to be similar to any other school crossing that I'd worked before. First to arrive at about 8.30am were, usually, giggling girls and these were followed by small groups of both boys and girls, chattering away without a care in the world. All the kids were smiling and polite until it got to the 'late for school, raggy-tag brigade' who arrived at about 9.05am. Some of them looked as though they'd just climbed out of bed with hair all over the place, still trying to fasten their shirt buttons and tripping over their shoe laces.

The last lad of all looked to be in a sorry state. The poor lad was wearing glasses with one of the lenses covered by sticking plaster to combat 'lazy eye' and his head was covered in a blue substance to cure ringworm. I felt really sorry for him and gave him some of my Spangle sweets. Just as I was about to go one of the teachers came to tell me that the lollipop lady I was covering for, had earlier visited the doctors and was now okay to do the dinnertime and teatime crossings. She also thanked me for my help.

From there I drove to the city and after dropping off the paperwork at the solicitors, I drove back along Effingham Road towards Attercliffe and hopefully my second pot of tea. I pulled up outside the premises of Mills Haulage near the top of Woodburn Road with the intention of having a pot of tea with Lawrence and Pat Mills, the owners.

As I got out of the car I was looking towards the city skyline when suddenly, about three quarters of a mile in front of me, I heard by far the loudest explosion that I'd ever heard. At the same time, I felt a tremor under my feet and then watched as a large orange glow appeared in the sky followed by an enormous black pall of smoke and debris shooting hundreds of feet into the air.

What the ---- was that, I thought, and for a few seconds I just stood there in stunned silence, watching the orange glow and the black cloud getting bigger and bigger. As I pulled myself together and came around a bit from the shock, I grabbed the radio and phoned Attercliffe nick to tell them what I'd witnessed and that I was going to investigate – my pot of tea would have to wait.

'We've heard the bang here, and if it's not in our division let the West Bar lads deal with it – do not attend, I repeat, do not attend,' said someone at the end of the office phone.

DO NOT ATTEND – DO NOT ATTEND! You must be ------- joking, I thought, as I jumped into the car, switched on the blue light and sped towards the plume of smoke. I inwardly used every swear word ever invented – how can you assess a situation when you're sat in an office two miles away? I set off cursing again, big style. I was absolutely livid – lives could be at risk.

Whatever had caused the huge blast was right in the heartland of the steelworks and somewhere, someone must be hurt I reasoned.

Racing down Worthing Road and then Lumley Street, I could see that the blast had caused people to come out of their houses and places of work to find out what was happening. There were loads of them, just standing there in shock. The cars had also stopped, and everyone was looking up into the air at the orange glow and the growing smoke plume.

Wherever the incident was I could see from the smoke, that I was getting nearer, and my concern now was that there had to be clear access for the fire brigade and possibly the ambulance – I had to be quick. I realized that from the time I first heard the explosion to now was only four or five minutes, which may well mean that I could be the first emergency service at the scene of the unknown incident.

At the small roundabout on Effingham Road, near to Tempered Springs Works on Leveson Street, I turned left towards the city and as I did so I stopped dead in my tracks.

I could see down the road for a distance of about a quarter of a mile and then the road disappeared round a left-hand bend. Spread out in front of me was a scene of utter devastation and carnage. There wasn't another uniform in sight and it was obvious that I was the first member of the emergency services to arrive at the scene – from this end of the city anyway.

On the left-hand side of the road, when facing the city, were about thirty parked cars all of which were squashed almost flat by heavy lumps of concrete. Was there anyone in the cars that needed rescuing? I didn't know. On the other side of the road were dozens of steel workers either standing or sitting on the pavement. The deadpan look on their faces told me that they were in a state of shock and had obviously vacated the nearby buildings after hearing the blast.

The above assessment of the situation had taken just seconds and I could also hear grit and dust landing on the metal roof of the Panda car, falling from the huge black cloud towering above us all.

I was out of the car now and questions were bouncing around in my head. Where the hell do I begin? What do I do first? Priorities, priorities, priorities. Everything looked to be a priority to me, so which one do you choose to deal with first?

Training schools, text books and advice from so-called experts don't help at all at times like this. Jobsworths sat behind a desk can all tell you what you should have done first, but only after the event! They are never there at the sharp end of the stick when it matters, and if they were here now they, themselves, having viewed the same scenes as me would be just like me – not knowing which way to jump.

As I looked behind me and back at the roundabout, I could see quite a crowd of blokes wondering what was going off, they'd obviously come from outside the impact area to look but didn't seem to be in shock. I hurriedly explained to them that I needed someone to stop vehicles from entering the road other than any emergency vehicles, and that I also needed help to create a pathway in order for those emergency vehicles to get through to the scene. They were all good men and, when I asked for volunteers to move some of the smaller pieces of concrete from the road, there was no shortage of willing helpers.

The concrete on top of the cars appeared to have come from a heavily-built concrete wall that had toppled over in the blast, pieces landing on top of the cars, so the road at that point was soon cleared, making way for ambulances and fire engines. Some of the concrete blocks must have come from elsewhere in the blast area and looked as if they could weigh maybe half a ton or more and they would obviously need lifting gear to remove them. Eventually a very rough path was created and with great difficulty it could be possible for fire and rescue to get through.

At that point I left my Panda car near the junction with its blue light flashing and concentrated on my next priority – was there anyone in the squashed cars? I bent down and quickly checked each one in turn and luckily, they were all empty, and must have belonged to the workers at nearby factories – thank goodness for that.

One of the things that I'll never forget that day was the eerie silence, everyone, including me, was in shock, no crying, no laughter, no shouting and bawling, just silence, it was uncanny.

As I started to walk nearer to the assumed blast site itself, I could see several people on the pavement who must have been injured by flying debris. From my arrival at the scene to now would have been probably five to six minutes and I could already hear sirens approaching the area from different parts of the city. What a relief.

I still hadn't seen another uniform but just as I was getting closer to the assumed point of the blast, I was met by a flustered looking fireman whose uniform suggested that he was of a high rank. He introduced himself, and I might be wrong, but I thought he said that his name was Reaney, or something similar.

'What the hell's happened here?' I could see from looking at him that he was probably a bit like me, not knowing what to do next.

'There are, unfortunately, four people dead, including the man over there,' he said; and he pointed to a gasometer where it could be seen that a body was hanging off railings.

'But what's caused the explosion in the first place?'

His next words to me will be forever stamped in my brain.

'It would appear that the blast has been caused with a welding torch igniting gas in an underground chamber with, believe it or not, three feet of concrete covering it! The main problem that I now have is that there is a possibility of another explosion and, if that happens, it will be more devastating than the first one. Can you please evacuate everyone from the area, just in case?'

Then he turned and walked away.

For a few seconds I was rooted to the spot and couldn't believe what he'd just said to me. Looking at the damage the first explosion had caused and then the thoughts of an even bigger one, I just couldn't take it in and wished that my trousers were brown and not blue at the thoughts of it.

A fire engine had arrived by now along with an ambulance and both must have been able to negotiate the road as they had arrived from the Attercliffe side of the explosion. As I looked back towards the roundabout I could see that everyone had mucked in together, just like they would have done in the war. I could see a forklift truck, a dumper truck and a small crane-type thing all helping to clear the road. What a wonderful team effort that was.

I pulled myself out of the trance that I was in and questioned what the fire officer had said. Had I heard him right, did he really say that another explosion could happen and even bigger than the first? I just couldn't get my head round that at all.

There were more people than ever knocking about and now, with the help of other police officers who were also at the scene, we moved as many onlookers back towards Norfolk Bridge and Attercliffe as we could. The site was only accessible by entering through Attercliffe as I had done, or from the city centre itself and I could only assume that at the other side of the blast area there were other policemen, ambulancemen and firemen who were doing the same thing that we were doing, that is, evacuating the area.

As I looked around me I could now see that every window in the surrounding premises were all blown in. Huge lumps of concrete had been thrown across the road and over the canal and slammed into the the sides of the factories that lined the canal bank.

The same thing had happened, believe it or not, with a JCB and that was also embedded in the wall of the factory at the other side of the canal.

We'd done all we could to move people away to safety from, what looked like a war zone. The silence was now deafening as there was nobody about at our side of the disaster site.

We were still in a nerve-racking situation, even though we were a quarter of a mile away from the scene, and as I stood in an entry, I lit a fag. The adrenaline rush was now subsiding, and I started to think through what had happened. Unfortunately, four people were dead, and my heart went out to their families. I also knew that had the blast happened at lunchtime when most of the steelworkers and business people would stand on the pavement outside the works, eating their fish and chips, etc; then scores and scores of people would have, most likely, been killed. I also thought about the firemen doing their job and how brave they must be, still working at the site with the full knowledge that there might be another explosion bigger than the last one. Speaking as a member of the public, I think you'll agree that we are all lucky to have people like that and all the other emergency services taking care of us.

I also thought about my wife Christine and the kids and the fact that had I driven down Effingham Road a quarter of an hour later than I did that morning, I quite easily could have been body number five. It was a horrible tragedy, but there could so easily be a lot more people killed. At that point, and I don't care who knows it, I quietly shed a few tears for everyone concerned that day.

A few hours later, with thankfully nothing else happening and the fact that the whole of the incident was being dealt with by the police of the West Bar Division, I headed back to the nick, dropped off the Panda car and went home.

I gave Christine and the kids a huge hug and we all had tea together.

The day after I was told that about thirty people had been taken to hospital as a result of the blast and some were more seriously injured than others. About sixty cars in total had been damaged beyond repair.

The explosion had been caused when a disused million-gallon petroleum tank in which town gas was once stored below ground, had been filled with water to cleanse it of anything flammable. Unfortunately, something wasn't quite right (don't ask me what, I don't know) but as soon as the workman got to work with his welding torch the whole thing went up in the air. What a catastrophe and I paid a silent tribute to the emergency services who had dealt with similar things to this in Sheffield in World War Two.

A few days later I had a walk around the area which was, of course, out of our division. Near the North Pole pub, I saw a street-name sign on one of the walls and I couldn't believe that the lane was called of all things BLAST LANE – how ironic is that. I often called in at Darnall fire station for a cup of tea and a week later I did just that. During a chat with Keith Foulds, one of the firemen, I discovered that he was big pals with my mate Jim Fletcher, a damn good copper. He then amazed me by telling me that the fourth person working at the blast site had nipped out to buy a sandwich just before the blast happened – how lucky was that?

'What about this then?' said Keith and he then continued, 'on that tall building at the other side of the road, and also the canal, was a window cleaner high up on the roof about to start his work. When the explosion happened, he was blown across the roof and knocked unconscious. All the windows in the building were broken, and the building was immediately evacuated. No one knew that he was there, until the following day when his wife, who didn't know where he was working, reported him missing. Someone must have put two and two together and, after the building was searched, he was found on the roof – injured but not seriously. What an escape!'

That meant that now three and not four men had lost their lives.

At a later inquest the coroner recorded the three victims as 'accidental deaths'. Will I and lots more people ever forget that day? I think not.

CHAPTER 15

Life's Ups and Downs

Before the Tinsley viaduct was erected there was no M1 section of the motorway going from Sheffield to Leeds. All the traffic going in a northerly direction came off the M1 at either Tinsley or Aston. At that point the drivers had to thread their way through the city and join the A57 road to Manchester or Liverpool. If motorists wanted to travel towards Barnsley, Wakefield, Leeds or Huddersfield they had to go through Hillsborough or Chapeltown. It was a nightmare journey for the drivers and at times a nightmare for us as we tried to keep the traffic running smoothly.

In order to alleviate the traffic problems, it was decided to build a new road called the Sheffield Parkway, creating a dual carriageway from a new roundabout at Catcliffe right into the city centre. What a mammoth task that was. With its many raised up flyover bridges and footbridges over its five miles length, it seemed to take years to complete.

About two miles of the proposed Parkway was due to pass through our division which at times we knew would cause problems. On Handsworth Road they would have to build a roundabout and then about twenty-five feet above that roundabout was going to be one of the flyovers. Prince of Wales Road, however, which was already a dual carriageway in parts was designed differently. Unlike Handsworth Road, three-quarters of a mile away, the Parkway here would go under the existing road and a large new roundabout was to be put in place above the new routeway.

Writing the previous chapter, reminded me of some incidents that happened during the Parkway's construction. See what you think.

When I patrolled my beat at Handsworth during the first part of the construction, a temporary roundabout was put in place. After that, convoys of tipper lorries started to dump piles of earth on the roundabout itself and it was obvious to locals that that was the precursor to building the flyover.

On this particular occasion I was working the 11pm to 7am nightshift. It was snowing, and no one was knocking about, but nevertheless I had to check all the shops and offices around Darnall to make sure that they were secure, and none had been broken into.

All the properties were okay and with still nobody knocking about I nipped into my mate Ike Worrall's bakery at the back of his shop on Main Road. Ike was a grafter and worked six nights a week producing bread and confectionery of all descriptions for his shop. I took off my helmet and jacket and put on a large white apron, and while I waited for the bell to ring on the oven I made us both a pot of tea. Eventually the bell rang, telling us that the loaves were now ready. Wearing protective gloves, I opened the door and retrieved, with the use of a long-handled paddle, all the loaves out of the oven. The smell of newly baked bread was fantastic. At the same time as I took the loaves out Ike replaced them with another load that he'd prepared earlier. My next job, again with the help of the padded gloves was to bang the corner of each tin containing a loaf, onto the big table, this released the loaf and Ike then took them into the front of his shop ready for sale in a few hours' time. I know that I didn't take long but it got me a pot of tea and a fresh loaf to take home for the family. It had also saved Ike some time, which he always appreciated.

By now it was about 3.30am and time for my snap at the little police sub-station about 150 yards away, so I took of my apron and swapped it for my tunic, grabbed my helmet, exchanged cheerios and off I went.

The little sub-station would only accommodate three officers, but I was the only one working that night and wished I'd have put the two-bar electric fire on before I went out on patrol, because it was freezing. My favourite cold fish sandwiches, laced with a dash of tomato sauce, followed by two bananas, went down in minutes, and sitting on the chair, I folded my arms and leaned on the wall next to the fire to keep warm. Suddenly I could hear a knocking noise. I'd obviously fallen asleep and as I jumped up startled the knock came again but louder. Who the hell is that at 4.30 in the morning? I thought. When I opened the door, I couldn't believe my eyes as I saw a young chap of about 25 wearing drainpipe trousers, winkle-picker shoes and a suede jacket. He was covered in mud and was shaking like a rabid dog; his teeth were chattering, and I could see that he was obviously frozen. I took him into the snap room, sat him in front of the fire and made him a pot of sweet tea to bring him round.

'What's up, lad? What's the problem?'

The poor lad's teeth were still chattering.

'My car is stuck on the top of a big pile of earth at Handsworth and I don't know how to get it off.'

I obviously knew which pile of earth that he was on about.

'How did you manage to get it stuck up there?'

'I skidded on the snow and lost control.'

'Are you injured?'

'No but I was lucky.'

'Right, when you've finished your tea we'll go and have a look and see what we can do.'

The poor lad was still shaking, so I found him an old police greatcoat and let him wear that. He looked just like a chocolate bobby and I had to laugh.

I was surprised at how much snow had fallen since I'd gone in for my snap, but we eventually managed to get to the roundabout and the large mound of earth, which must have been about twenty feet high. I couldn't see the car and couldn't reckon up where it was. It just reminded me of Chapter 5 in my first book, *What's Tha up to?* where a car had also skidded and spiraled high up into the air, it was amazing.

I could see the tyre marks in the snow, snaking their way up the slope, but I still couldn't see his car.

'Where the hell is this car of yours?'

The lad looked as perplexed as I was and started to climb the slippery slope, at the same time saying, 'It was up there, but now I can't see it.'

I felt like Edmund Hillary climbing Everest. My boots were covered in mud and the bottoms of my trousers were getting wet through, what a carry on, but eventually, I managed to get to the top.

'It must be down there,' he said.

'What do you mean it's down there, down where?' I said as I caught up with him.

Unbeknown to me or the lad, there was a wide trench which had been cut through the centre of the huge mound of earth. Looking down into the blackness with my torch I could see large wooden timbers shoring up the sides of what was, in effect, a channel through the mound, and right at the bottom was the poor lad's car. I couldn't believe my eyes, and neither could he.

Apparently, he'd travelled from Worksop and was on his way to a new job in Liverpool. At the time of his accident there was only light snow and with no one about he decided to put the car through its paces. He'd been on this road before but suddenly, in the darkness, he was met by the huge half-made roundabout, which caught him totally unawares. He hadn't had time to think and before he knew it, his fast speed had carried him to the top of the mound of earth. When he got out of the car, in the darkness, he noticed that the nose end of the car had been pointing slightly downhill, as if he was heading down the other side of the mound.

He told me that after leaving the car where it was he started to walk towards Darnall and was directed to the sub-station by a bloke waiting for his mate to take him to his early shift at the steelworks.

There was nothing else we could do at the accident site so we went back to the sub-station and it was still freezing cold, so we warmed ourselves up with a pot of tea, and as we spoke about what had happened we decided that the heat of the engine must have softened the mud and snow and the weight of the engine at the front of the car had tipped it forward and it must have slowly slid down and into the trench.

He'd had a lucky escape that day but unlucky as I had to report him for careless driving! I often wondered how the job in Liverpool went or if he even got there.

By now it was time for the morning shift to come in, so I handed the job and the lad over to them and thankfully went home to my warm house and to bed.

Unfortunately, incident number two didn't have such a happy ending.

After what seemed like an eternity the new Parkway was now nearing completion. The Prince of Wales Road roundabout was now complete and when you drove around it you could see below it the new road taking shape. Workmen, dumper lorries and cranes were everywhere. The new footbridge near to the entrance of the now old Parkway market, had not long been completed. It looked great and had been built in separate concrete sections which spanned the new road.

Towards teatime one day I got a call to stop any traffic from entering onto the new road from the roundabout itself, which I thought was rather odd as it wasn't yet opened to the public. A minute later I got another call telling me that as well as stopping traffic on the road I must allow swift access down the newly created slip road which gave access to the carriageway, for any emergency vehicles as there had been a nasty accident near the old Sheffield Parkway market.

With the blue light flashing, I sped to the location, got out on the roundabout and looked towards the scene of the accident. I could see two blue lights flashing and I could tell from the make of the fast cars, that it was F Division (road traffic division).

As I looked again I couldn't believe my eyes. One of the concrete spans of the footbridge was now missing and beneath it was one of the dumper trucks, but from where I was I couldn't tell what had happened. I'd been at the scene for maybe a minute when both a fire engine and ambulance arrived together. I made sure that the workers' vehicles were lined up at the sides of the carriageway to ensure that the emergency vehicles could get immediate access.

Fortunately for me, I had nothing to do with the accident itself but was later told that one of the dumper truck drivers, who was on his last run of the day, having tipped his last load, had innocently forgotten to lower the back of the lorry which had been left sticking upright in the air. Probably, in his excitement of going home, the poor man hadn't noticed this. The back of the truck was now pointing upwards instead of being level and hit one section of the concrete bridge, which dragged that part of the bridge along with it and the massive concrete slab fell onto the cab of the lorry, crushing the two men inside it. The poor men wouldn't have known a thing as it had happened too fast. The lorry was there for a couple of days before specialist lifting equipment was able to lift the concrete slab.

How unlucky they were, hard workers and just a split-second lack of concentration.

At about midnight, during Christmas week, I'd started night shift at 11pm and would finish at 7am. I'd made a promise to Christine's aunty and uncle, Joan and Harry Dallamore, who lived at 601 Prince of Wales Road, the nearest house to the now, recently opened Parkway. They were having a family Christmas party and, unfortunately, because I was working, Christine and I couldn't be there, but I'd promised them that if I had the chance I'd nip in. What a cracking family they were. Christine's cousins Glen and Jennifer, who were always good for a laugh, along with some of Joan and Harry's workmates were also there. I obviously couldn't partake of any of the liquid refreshment that they were offering me and settled for a pot of tea. The food was delicious, and I'd have loved to have stayed.

Shortly before midnight I grudgingly left the house with all its Christmas 'spirit' and as I pulled the car out of the drive

I was, as near as damn it, on the Prince of Wales roundabout itself. As I approached the far side, where the exit road comes in from the Parkway, a car shot straight out of the slip road. I quickly swung the police car to the right, or otherwise he would have hit me sideways on, and he just managed to stop. What the bloody hell is that nutter up to, I thought as I jumped out of the car, switched the engine off and left the blue light on. I grabbed the door of his car and pulled it open, I was that mad. A middle-aged man was driving the car with his wife sat at the side of him and two little children in the back seat, and there was a strong smell of alcohol.

'What the hell are you playing at mate, you nearly rammed me?' I yelled, 'how many pints have you had?'

'T... t... t ... t ... two,' he said, which obviously wasn't true. The man's wife was looking at me with tears in her eyes and out of sight of her husband she had a resigned look on her face as if to say, he's had more than that love, you know he has. So, I asked him again, 'I've given you the chance to tell me the truth, I'm now going to ask you for the second time. How many pints have you had?'

He finally managed to say 'two' again. I wasn't pleased to say the least and I asked him what he did for a living, and his wife answered tearfully, 'He's a lorry driver love, we've only come from my mums at Handsworth and I told him not to drive and to get a taxi, but he wouldn't have it.'

'Where do you live?' I asked, and again his poor wife answered. 'Dawlands Close, love.'

As I looked at the man again, I could see fear in his eyes as he'd obviously understood his situation. I cautioned him and told him that I was arresting him on suspicion of drink driving and told him that I was going to take him to my car to give him a breathalyzer test.

By this time, we all carried breathalyzer kits in the police car. So, putting the separate units together, I attached it to the plastic bag and asked him to take a big breath and blow into it. We were standing in front of the police car at this stage and as I retrieved the glass phial from the kit I watched the crystals inside changing from yellow to green. If the crystal passed a line marked on the phial, then he was over the limit. He was over the limit all right and I showed him the tube in the light from the headlights and his face was ashen, and tears were streaming down his cheeks. Because I was still angry, I once more asked him what he did for a living and he muttered, 'Lorry driver.'

'I thought that's what your wife told me. Do you realize that you have just lost your job? You're under arrest.' I sat him in the police car and locked the doors so that he couldn't escape.

When I got back to his car both the lady and the two children were crying and she was distraught. I told her what had happened.

'It's his own stupid fault, he's a good man officer, we've had a tough time lately. His dad's just passed away, and he's been out of work for six months and has just got this new job as a lorry driver. He shouldn't have done this but even though I told him to, I knew we couldn't afford a taxi.'

Like every copper in the country I was used to sob stories, some people tried it on, but you got hardened to it. What a bloody idiot. He'd driven to his mother-in-law's house only a mile away and then driven back to within a quarter of a mile of his own house, told me lies and he'd nearly hit the police car as well. What was I to do? The other side of the picture though, was that I believed what his wife had said to me. She was distraught, knowing what was what. His kids were crying, and it was also Christmas.

In those days there were nowhere near as many cars as there are today, so I made my decision and opened the car door again to speak to his wife.

'We all have tough times in life, love, and we've all done silly things. I think he's been taught a lesson tonight and I know that you'll give him some ear ache. You stay here with the kids.'

'Why,' she said through the tears, 'are you taking him to prison?'

'No, I'm going to take him home and then come back to fetch you and the kids – it's my Christmas gift to you all.'

At that point she started to cry all over again.

His car was safely parked, so I walked back to the police car, hoping that I was doing the right thing. I unlocked the doors and as I got in I could see that he was sobbing; but what the hell was that smell – and then it hit me. The man didn't know that I was letting him off the hook and making sure that he didn't lose his license as a lorry driver and he was obviously terrified at the thoughts of what he'd done and what would happen, so much so, and to put it bluntly, he'd bloody shit himself!

With windows fully down, I drove as fast as I could on the quarter of a mile journey and he let himself into his house. I asked him for a peg to put on my nose, but he was in such as state that the request went over his head.

When I got back to the car I bundled his wife and the kids into the police car, apologizing for the smell as I whispered to her what had happened, and after locking his car up I dropped them back at their home.

Out of the three incidents I referred to on the Parkway, I think you'll agree that he was the luckiest of them all.

A few weeks after this he found me out and came to apologize by saying:

'Thank you so much for what you did for me and also for my family that night and I can assure you, honestly, that that will never ever happen again.'

I could tell that he meant every word.

Even today, and every time I get near to that roundabout, I start to sniff the air thinking about that night and always have a chuckle to myself. Hadn't he been lucky?

CHAPTER 16

Roman Coins and Rock and Roll

What a cracking day. The sun was out for the first time in about two weeks and to make matters better it was my day off work. I'd promised the kids that we could have breakfast in a café somewhere, so at about 7am we were ready for off on a family day out with a difference. Flasks, a picnic, a bunch of bananas, a toilet roll (in case someone was taken short in the middle of a field); and metal detectors and spades were all packed away in the boot. Our first stop was the café near to the Beckingham roundabout on the Gainsborough road. After what was always a smashing breakfast consisting of eggs, bacon, black pudding, fried bread and beans we were ready for off. The kids had a little spade each and were really excited at the thoughts of finding buried treasure.

I was into history and fascinated by the Roman occupation of England. We were out for the day to literally do some 'digging' and I had to chuckle as I remembered my very first treasure hunting days.

When I was a 7-year-old lad, I accidentally found a large hoard of Roman coins in the bottom of a builder's trench. Not realizing what they were, my mate Roy and I played with them and threw them everywhere, until a policeman pulled us out of the trench, which frightened us both stupid. Somebody called an 'archaeologist' (which meant nothing to me), came and took the coins away. Much later on I realized just what we'd found, and I was forever hooked on Roman history, and found it absolutely fascinating.

I was looking through *Exchange and Mart* one day in 1964 when I spotted an advert for Joan Allen's Electrical Company in Biggin Hill in Kent. The advert showed a picture and the description was: 'Find metal underground with this Metal Detector'. The device looked a bit like what the sappers used during the war when searching for unexploded bombs. How exciting, I thought.

I ordered one immediately, much to Christine's annoyance as we were saving up to get married and to put a deposit on a house. The machine duly arrived, and I couldn't wait to take it out on its first foray in order for me to find my fortune. I was certain that this was the way forward in making us rich.

When Christine and I were courting, being in the police force meant that my days off didn't always fall on a weekend. The first weekend that coincided with Christine's was the ideal opportunity for us to have a day out together. Christine wanted to go hiking in Derbyshire, to make the most of the sunshine, finishing off in the Millstone pub for tea and then a slow drive home taking in the lovely countryside – but I had different ideas!

Much to Christine's annoyance we set off on our first outing with the metal detector. We hadn't gone far when I spotted an opening in the hedge and thought it would be an ideal place to test out my new 'toy'. Out of the boot of the car came the metal detector and spade. We turned the machine on and it gave a beep, beep, which meant that the batteries were working okay. Excitedly I started walking up and down with the dectector just a few inches above the ground, when all of a sudden, a loud screech came from the machine and we both jumped out of our skin. Bingo – we'd hit gold, or so I thought. Christine dug a hole right under where the detector had made the loud screech and after we'd dug a couple of inches down, I passed the detector over the hole, and again a louder screech this time. We kept digging but still we hadn't reached the 'metal'. This had to be something special – a treasure chest full of gold coins perhaps, roman jewellery that someone had hidden and forgotten about, there were endless possibilities. We didn't give up and after about four hours of hard work we'd reached the metal. Carefully scraping the earth away from it, we'd found four feet of railway lines! Christine wasn't pleased at all and we went home in stony silence.

Eventually, after a few months I was that fed up with it, that I threw the bloody machine into a swamp and I hoped that someone else found it in a thousand years' time, placing it in a museum.

Since the days of that first metal detector, machines have got much better and I had purchased a newer model. I'd used it before and it was absolutely brilliant, but I was only finding Victorian pennies, shillings and the odd threepenny 'dodger'. It proved that the machine was good, but I wanted to find the older stuff such as Roman or Medieval. I'd heard that the best place to find Roman coins was in Lincolnshire where the soil was lighter and could be farmed easier than the heavy clay soil where we lived. The other reason why the Romans both lived and worked the land in Lincolnshire was because of the River Trent. This provided water to irrigate the crops and it was also part of the trading route for various commodities, such as lead and grinding stones going from England to Rome. The ships, on their return to England, would bring back with them such things as wine, olives, olive oil and spices among other things. There wasn't much point in metal detecting the land if no one had lived or worked on it, as there would be no casual metal losses such as coins or artifacts.

I was quite excited as my good friend John Harris had just gained permission to search a load of land in Lincolnshire and he'd invited me down for the day. I couldn't believe my luck and now we were nearly there I couldn't wait to see him. The kids were now getting restless and needed to have a good run out in the fresh air.

On our arrival, John was already talking to the farmer and his wife who owned the land. They were a smashing couple and we agreed to show them everything that we'd found.

They then pointed us towards a large number of fields. They were absolutely enormous, and it would have taken us years and years to search them properly.

John Harris was a great guy and also extremely knowledgeable, and when it came to electronics he was an absolute wizard. He worked for lots of different film companies, both in this country and overseas and a few years later he did lots of the special effects for the television show *London's Burning*.

I'd first met him at a metal detecting rally in North Yorkshire a few weeks earlier. There were a lot of people there that day and we all took up positions and surrounded the perimeter of a very large ploughed field. At the appointed start time everyone started detecting. The large group had only been detecting for about forty minutes when suddenly we were all called off the field by panicking stewards. At the far corner, high up on the slope, two people had, independently, each found a hand grenade. We hung about for a bit while the police arrived and sent for the bomb disposal team from York. We were later told that the previous farmer must have been paid to bury them after the Second World War and there were several crates full of grenades which were later blown up in a controlled explosion. What a wasted journey, John had found a Victorian penny and I'd found nothing.

On this occasion we were hoping for a better day, Christine had taken the kids for a walk so John and I, unsure of where to start, set off slowly swinging our detectors from side to side.

All of a sudden, we heard a loud bang as if someone had fired a shotgun. Both John and I stopped but we couldn't see where the noise had come from. It was a bit of a concern, but we had permission to be there, so we didn't consider ourselves to be in any danger. Half an hour later the same thing happened again, which was odd. By this time, having found very little on the first field, we moved onto a different one, which we hoped would produce something better.

We were nearer to each other now and as we slowly walked up the slope towards the wood I saw John stop and start digging and a second later he held his hand up in the air and shouted: 'Coin Martyn, Roman bronze.'

Wow, if nothing else turned up that day, then that one coin that John had found was worth the journey. Ten minutes later, it was my turn to jump up and down excitedly as I'd also found another 2,000-year-old Roman bronze coin. Unbelievable – to think that roughly 2,000 years ago a Roman soldier, farmer or child had lost something so small. Once more we heard the bang but still couldn't see anybody and carried on detecting. In the space of an hour and a half, John had found eight more coins and I'd found six. I was ecstatic and wanted to show Christine and the kids, but they were nowhere in sight.

Time for a natter and a fag. We both walked over to a large wooden gatepost and sat down with our back to the hedge whilst examining our coins. We couldn't believe our luck. In the next instance there was a huge bang immediately behind us and we both jumped up in a panic, and I can't write here the language that was used. We still couldn't see anybody, but on looking behind the gatepost there was a contraption which we realized was a gas gun, or bird scarer, or for that matter, a people scarer, to stop poaching.

Once we knew what it was we weren't worried anymore and we settled down for ten minutes with a flask and a fag.

So, once more we set off detecting. Within a few yards I found another Roman coin but this time it was a silver denarius which had the emperor's head of Hadrian on the reverse side of it. It was like winning the pools and I was on cloud nine. We were obviously on a decent spot, so I beckoned Christine and the kids across to me to let them have a try with the detector. They couldn't wait. With a little bit of help because of their size, Sally found two coins and Richard and Christine one each and they were quite excited. In total John had found a total of thirteen bronze coins and three silver, whereas I'd only found eight bronze and one silver.

At this point it started to drizzle with rain and having had a fabulous day out with the kids and knowing that we had to be home early as we were having visitors, we set off back. I wanted to look at the coins that Richard and Sally had found but I had to prize them out of their fingers almost because they didn't want to let go of them.

Within minutes of our journey home Christine and the kids were fast asleep, the fresh air, away from the city had done us all good.

When we arrived home, I was dying to soak the coins in water just to see what they were like. It's a sobering thought to think that we'd dug something out of the ground that someone had last handled 2,000 years ago. Who did they belong to and what were they like? Would they have been gutted to lose their coins? All these questions run through your mind when you find coins and artifacts and it is always thrilling. The value of the bronze ones was very little and the rough condition of the silver one, not much better. It's the history rather than the value that is so exciting about metal detecting and you never get bored with it. But you never know, one day we might strike it rich.

The following day, I was supposed to be working the 8am to 4pm shift and there was a rumour that I might have to work later because of a football match at Sheffield Wednesday football ground. Most of our lads loved going to the football because they were able to watch the match for free, but I wasn't one of them, as I loved cricket. When we got home from our day out metal detecting, a note had been pushed through the door from the boss telling me that instead of going to the football match, I was to work a 3pm to 11pm shift up in the city centre. He didn't elaborate as to why, but I was just pleased that I didn't have to attend the game.

I reported for duty at West Bar police station and was surprised to see several other policemen there, also from Attercliffe, and some others from Woodseats Division. Amongst the Woodseats lads I could see my mate Jim

Fletcher, a bloody good bobby who I'd had plenty of laughs with.

'What are we doing up town Jim, any ideas?'

'I was going to ask you the same question, I've no idea. There are about forty of us here and we've got to wait for a briefing from the boss. So we're all going up to the canteen for a pot of tea until we're sent for.'

And off we went.

About an hour later, we were all called together and addressed by the Chief Inspector. 'Good afternoon, gentlemen. Sorry to take you all away from your normal duties but we've got a concert going off later at the City Hall, which isn't unusual at all and we can usually cope with these things. Our problem is that a few nights ago this same pop group played at another venue in Manchester and the Manchester Police have informed us that we may need to be aware of mass hysteria taking place.'

Some bright spark, shouted, 'Is that the name of the pop group, Sir?' and everybody laughed.

'Very funny – no the pop group is called the Bay City Rollers, whoever they are.'

You could tell by the puzzled look on everyone's faces, including mine, that no one had heard of them.

'Apparently, gents, they have a huge following of young girls and tickets are like gold dust. They were sold out in no time, just like at Manchester and we've also been warned that there might be gatecrashers desperately wanting to get in to see their 'heart throbs'. So just to be sure, we've drafted you gents in to keep an eye on things. It should be a pretty low-key event, so if you make your way up to the City Hall, we'll take it as it comes. The Bay City Rollers will be taken to the venue in the back of a police transit van and sneaked in through the side door. That's all lads. Thank you. See you all up there.'

The City Hall was about a third of a mile away and Jim and I along with the others ambled up there to monitor the situation. What an amazing sight, hundreds of young girls milling about around the Hall. Most of them were wearing tartan hats and scarves and were all eagerly awaiting the arrival of the group. We just mingled amongst them to make our presence felt and to try and keep everyone calm. Amazingly some of the fans had travelled from all over the British Isles just to see their idols. Some of the kids had tickets but a lot of them were there hoping that there were some spare, but it was obvious that there wouldn't be enough (if there were any at all) for the huge amount of kids wanting them. Manchester police were right, and the developing situation needed keeping an eye on.

When the van arrived containing the group there was a huge surge forward, everyone wanted a glimpse of the lads as they went into the building and the noise from the screaming girls was deafening. What an amazing sight. The main doors were opened and the girls with tickets were let in, but we all felt sorry for the poor fans who were unable to be admitted. The City Hall held over two thousand people but even after the lucky ticket holders had gone in there were still hundreds left outside.

When the concert started all the girls outside could just about hear the music and they all started dancing. Some of the policemen were joining in and so was I, the party atmosphere was infectious, it was brilliant and there wasn't a bit of trouble.

Eventually the concert finished, and the girls started to pour out of the building and into the fresh air. It was still a great atmosphere and it had obviously been a great night for the kids, but then as we were watching from a short distance away and much to our astonishment, we saw first one of the girls slump onto the floor, then another and another. They were dropping like flies, it was incredible to see – it was then that I realized what mass hysteria was. The girls were attended to by the St John's Ambulance Brigade who were always on stand-by at this kind of event and were used to dealing with this sort of thing. What a wonderful job they do, and without the recognition that they deserve. The girls recovered quite quickly and still there was no trouble.

When things had died down a bit one of the police transit vans pulled up to take us back to West Bar. A group of girls must have thought that the van contained the Bay City Rollers being secretly moved from the City Hall and we were surrounded by screaming fans. We couldn't move, and it was only when we opened the back door of the van so that they could see inside it, that they left, and we were able to move on. Its not very often that you will find a van load of coppers singing *Bye Bye Baby, Baby Bye Bye* at the tops of their voices. It had turned out to be a memorable and enjoyable shift and one that none of us will ever forget.

CHAPTER 17

'A Bobby's Job'

Y
ou've got a 'bobby's job' pal – has been said to me on umpteen occasions throughout my time on the beat. My reply back was always the same, 'You're right, I love it but at times it's not much COP!'

I've always been up for a laugh and working weekends down the Cliffe on my own on a Friday or Saturday night, when people had had a few too many, meant that a situation could go either way dependent on how you dealt with it. I found that the best way was to join in with the laughter and thus avoid confrontation, but it didn't always work.

Girls on a night out and after they'd had one or two drinks became brave and used to goad me with comments like: 'Is that a tit on your head?' or 'Have you got a pointed head?'; or 'I bet you've got a big truncheon'; or 'Can I feel your truncheon?'; or 'I've always wanted to kiss a copper'. I'd heard them all time and time again, but I always tried to make a joke of it and laugh along with them.

The blokes were different, and they'd say things like: 'What time is it officer?'

'It's time you bought a bloody watch'.

'Do you live in a police station?'

'No, I live on Letsby Avenue' (think about it lets – be – having – you). The trouble with the blokes was that there was always one. Even before you saw him you could stake your life on the fact that he would be 5 foot and a tab end tall, with more fat on a cold chip and a mouth like a parish oven with t'door open. The smallest blokes were all the same and if 'Mr Mouth Almighty' flexed his muscles when trying to be clever, his vest would fall off. You knew that his first comment, when squaring up for a fight, would be something like, 'I hate you ------- coppers', and everybody would look at me for my reactions.

Years ago, when a similar thing first happened to me, I grabbed the lad and arrested him, which caused uproar amongst his mates and several of them had to be locked up as well. That night taught me a lesson and thereafter, when I found myself in a similar situation, I used a different tactic. My reply was always the same, 'I don't blame you mate, some of 'em can be bastards, I'm on your side.' Everybody would laugh at my unexpected reply and suddenly we were all pals together again. No one hurt – no one locked up – no animosity. As I've said before, better to work with people than against them, was my motto.

The funny thing is that people remember occasions like that, and at times when I found myself in trouble, people would side with me as opposed to their pals and it was one of the reasons why I enjoyed working the beat so much, but you didn't know from one minute to the next what was going to happen.

I'd started work at Attercliffe at 8am and walked down Attercliffe Road to Bodmin Street where I was about to do my favourite job which was taking the kids across the road to start their day at Huntsman Gardens School. I loved chatting with the kids and their mums and sometimes, but very rarely, their dads. There was loads of work in those days and the dads were mostly at work in the steelworks. As usual some of the kids were early, nearly always girls and the kids on the last push were usually lads.

You had to be on your toes at this busy time of day as the traffic was none stop. The other reason you had to be attentive was that in 1968 Sheffield and Rotherham police forces amalgamated and the Chief Constable of Rotherham now became the Deputy Chief Constable of Rotherham and Sheffield. He was based in Rotherham and came through Attercliffe every morning to get to his office in Sheffield. As he drove past he expected you to salute him, what a pillock. I always pretended not to see him!

After I'd taken the main rush of kids across the road, I gave it another five minutes so that I could make sure that any stragglers were safely across and I then made my way to the junction of Staniforth Road and Attercliffe Road to where the old police box was.

Just before I got to the police box I could hear an emergency siren, the noise of which was getting louder as it came towards me. A few seconds later I saw the ambulance in the distance, so I jumped into the middle of the road with a view to stopping the traffic to let the emergency vehicle through. Was he going to turn right or go straight on? I didn't know. A few seconds later I realized that he must be going straight on because at that speed he would never have been able to turn right, so I stopped the traffic coming down Staniforth Road to allow him to go straight through the junction at speed.

When he'd safely gone through I nipped into the police box and had a crafty fag. Just as I finished, the phone in the police box went and the sergeant asked me to attend Dr Foggitt's surgery which was about a quarter of a mile away, near the end of Worksop Road and right next to the Palace Theatre.

Apparently, a man had collapsed in the surgery, and an ambulance had been sent for, obviously the same one that I'd let through, but it was too late to save him. If the man had been alive and conveyed to hospital and later passed away there, it would have been dealt with by them, but, because he'd died before the ambulance arrived, it was our duty to deal with the body and by the time I got there the ambulance had left the scene. Walking into the surgery, I could see the body on the floor covered with a blanket.

I couldn't make my mind up whether to inwardly chuckle or feel sorry for the poor people waiting to be seen by the doctor. It couldn't have been very pleasant for them to have witnessed what had happened and they all looked very grim faced as they were waiting for their turn.

Dr Foggitt had already certified the death but not the cause, as he hadn't treated the man for some time and so for that reason, I had to call for the mortuary van to come and remove the body to the mortuary in Nursery Street. Luckily for the poor patients in the surgery, the van arrived about fifteen minutes later, and with the body in the mortuary van, off we went. Because I'd gone in the van with the mortuary attendant I had no means of transport, so I had to ring the office and arranged to meet PC Les Igoe, who had arrived to pick me up.

It being daytime, the attendant removed the clothing and placed it in a neat pile. I'd already got the man's details from Dr Foggitt's secretary and Les and I then had the horrible task of going to tell the poor man's wife, a job we all hated.

The poor old lady, for obvious reasons, took it very badly and to make matters worse for her, we had to take her to the mortuary to identify and confirm that it was indeed her husband. She was more than upset and we allowed her a few minutes on her own with her dead husband before we took her back home, but before we did so, we collected the man's belongings and put them in a bag for her.

Back at her home in Darnall, we couldn't just dump her with the bag of her husband's clothes, so we did what we usually did in such circumstances and we made her a cup of tea with plenty of sugar in it. By us all having a pot of tea and staying with her for about fifteen minutes, it allowed her to do a lot of crying and also tell us about her husband, which we hoped would help her a bit. We went back to Attercliffe police station and after writing up a sudden-death report, I ate my snap; and after a quick game of snooker with Les, I was back out on the beat again.

Just as I got to Attercliffe Baths corner, I heard someone shout my name and looking across the road I saw that it was Frank from the antiques shop where I sometimes called for a pot of tea with his wife May. He was beckoning me across the road and as I went into the shop he said, 'I've got something here that might interest you, Martyn,' and pointed to an American rocking chair. These rocking chairs were the first flat-packed furniture to be exported to England and beyond, at the turn of the century.

'Why would that interest me, Frank?'

'I know you're interested in antiques. It's not the chair, it's the silver plaque on the front of the chair seat that I wanted you to see.'

So, helmet off, I bent down to look and the inscription read:

Presented to
PC 230 Elijah Bell
By officers and men of Brightside Division
Sheffield City Police Force
After 26 years' service
April 2nd 1896

With me being into history I was blown away when I saw it, but I didn't show it, or the price would have gone up. There was no such thing as Brightside Division any more, but the most exciting thing for me was that in the 1870s and 1880s one of my maternal great uncles had a farm in Brightside. What a coincidence, they must have known each other. I couldn't believe it and nonchalantly asked the price. It was £7, a fair amount of money back then.

'Blimey Frank, that's a lot of money. I'm not bothered about the chair, I'm only interested in the plaque (which was a white lie). I'd pay £4 for it but no more.'

'I'll tell you what I'll do,' said Frank. 'Give me £5 and I'll throw in his truncheon. They both came out of a house clearance in Pitsmoor.'

'Deal. Can I pay in instalments?'

Luckily for me he said that I could and a month later the chair was mine. I was well chuffed with it and we still have it today, and it's rocked my children and my grandchildren to sleep many times over the years.

After a pot of tea with Frank and May, I went out on patrol again and when I got back to the station to finish at 4pm Inspector Radford wanted to see me and Les again. What the hell's that about, we both thought.

'The wife of that dead man that you dealt with has just rang the office saying what a good job you both did in looking after her,' the Inspector said, and we both gave a smile, how nice. 'But there's a problem.'

'What's that, sir?' I asked.

'She said that her husband didn't feel very well this morning, so he decided to go to the doctors and at the same time he was going to call in at the travel agent to pay for their holidays. He took with him £110, (a lot of money in those days) and when his wife checked his clothing after you had gone, the money wasn't there.'

Les and I looked at each other with our mouths open and just as I was about to ask to be searched there and then by the Inspector, Les started to say the same thing. We couldn't believe it, I knew I hadn't got it, Les knew that he hadn't got it, at least I hoped he hadn't got it. What a bloody carry on. After searching us, and also the police car that we had travelled in at our insistence the inspector went first of all to the travel agent and then to take a statement off the lady. Les or I were too concerned, as the poor man had probably called to the agency before going to the doctors.

Unfortunately for us that wasn't the case, he hadn't paid any money in there, so now we were worried. It was the end of the shift and I went home and naturally I was worried sick. I'd known Les, who was an old timer, for several years and knowing that I hadn't got the money, I couldn't believe that he might have. I couldn't sleep that night and was glad that I hadn't paid any money to Frank for the chair, but instead was going to pay in instalments. That certainly would have looked suspicious for me.

The first thing I did when I got to work the following day was to see the inspector. The lady's statement he had taken categorically stated that she had given her husband the money herself as he was putting on his suit. No ifs, no buts. The inspector said that he'd been to the mortuary, interviewed the mortuary staff and also searched the mortuary van. There was nothing in the van and he was happy with the mortuary attendant's statement.

I met up with Les at snap time and he, like me, looked stressed out of his brains.

'I haven't got it Les.'

'And neither have I.'

So, we both, once more went to see the inspector, suggesting that the doctor's surgery should be checked out, along with the people in there. Neither of us were surprised when he told us that he'd already done that and the enquiry that he'd made there proved negative. The doctor didn't know anything and after getting a list of the patients waiting to be seen he'd visited them all and was satisfied that they also knew nothing about it.

Both Les and I were going frantic, two days turned to three and then to four. Neither of us could sleep and were worried sick, it was very frustrating. On the fifth day, I again asked the inspector if he'd heard anything from the lady.

'No, nothing at all Johnson.'

'Sir, when we took her home, she was seriously upset and, with a lot on her mind, could she have got it wrong. With your permission, sir, I'd like to go and see her myself, but preferably with you. Neither Les or I can sleep and its sending us both crackers.'

'Okay, if that's what you want but I don't think it'll do any good at all. Come on then, drive me up there and we'll have a chat with her,' he said.

After knocking on the door, it was opened by the lady and she recognised me and almost straight away said, 'I'm sorry about the trouble I've caused, and I was going to ring you, but I forgot.'

'What were you going to ring us about?' asked the inspector, and she looked at him and said, 'When you went the other day I decided to check his other clothes and I found the money in the inside pocket of another jacket. I was going to ring and tell you, but I've been so confused. I'm sorry, I forgot,' and she showed us the money. I have a great respect and love for old people as without them we wouldn't be here today, but I didn't know whether to laugh or cry at what she'd just said. What a bloody relief.

As we left the house there was steam coming out of the inspector's ears. All that trouble and effort made by him for nothing at all. Both Les and I were over the moon at the outcome and bore the old lady no animosity at all even though we both used a thousand swear words about what had happened over the last few days. We felt sorry for the lady, all ready for her holidays having saved up all year to visit a relative in America only for her hopes to be dashed. The inquest showed that her poor husband had died of a heart attack. No wonder she was confused.

When I got home that night Christine was obviously relieved when I told her the outcome. Along with the kids, we had tea together and after putting the kids to bed I was gagging for a pint, so I nipped next door to the Mason's Arms. After a few pints and a few games of crib with my mates, the banter and laughter made me feel better, and I went to bed knackered but happy and slept soundly for the next ten hours. Pressure off – what next? We never knew.

CHAPTER 18

Balls! And 'Mr Crowbar'

The church at Tinsley was a beautiful building and, rather unusually I thought, was dedicated to St Lawrence. Christine and I had been invited to the harvest festival service which was to be followed by tea in the vicarage garden. I'd met the vicar a couple of weeks earlier at the youth club in Darnall. I would often spend an hour or two at the club which was attended mainly by local teenagers. It was a way for us all to get to know each other better and it was surprising how glad some of them were to be able to confide in someone who would listen. The visiting vicar thought it was a brilliant idea and for that reason, he invited us and a member of the fire brigade to his church in Tinsley for a chat about doing a similar public relations exercise there. My mate Mick Plant, an excellent bobby, had recently become the Area Policeman covering Tinsley and he had also been invited.

It made a change for me and Christine to go to church and having got her mum Mabel, to baby sit, we were off. The service was brilliant and with the hymns *All Things Bright and Beautiful* followed by *We Plough the Fields and Scatter* it meant that we could all sing our hearts out.

Christine was chatting to a group of ladies, so on our arrival in the vicar's garden both Mick and I were gagging for a pot of tea after all the singing. We were both big lads and could have supped a river dry, it was such a warm day. Anybody, who knows me will tell you that I am a proper 'tea belly' and when I'm drinking either beer or tea I am a pint pot man. Whoever invented those delicate tiny cups and saucer things to drink out of wanted locking up, in my opinion.

With great ceremony the vicar's wife presented us both with a plate containing small salmon and cucumber sandwiches, even a sparrow could have eaten more. Next came our tea, in two tiny and fragile Royal Albert cups on top of an equally tiny and fragile saucer.

Both Mick and myself were there in a public relations capacity and for that reason we were both in full uniform. Allow me to set the scene. Two 6'1", heavily-built bobbies on a warm sunny afternoon, hungry and thirsty, standing facing each other in the middle of the vicarage lawn. A plate of tiny sandwiches in one hand, a poxy little cup and saucer in the other, with nowhere to put them. We were stuck and could neither eat nor drink. Wyatt Earp and Billy the Kidd would have been proud as we both stood opposite each other like a pair of gunslingers in a duel, unsure of what to do next.

Mick was like me and we could both see the funny side of the situation. I looked at him and he looked at me and our lips started curling up to form a smile. The smiles got bigger because of our predicament and then we both started to chuckle. Laughter, as we all know, is infectious and as I looked at Mick I could see that the more he chuckled the more his helmet was wobbling up and down, which made me chuckle even more. He of course could see my helmet wobbling up and down the same as his which made us both laugh. That's it, I thought, and we both started to laugh, uncontrollably. At this stage I could see that the tea in his cup was slopping into his saucer and his sandwiches were sliding about on his plate and with everybody watching us we'd now lost the plot and were totally out of control. Mick's cup fell off the saucer and luckily fell onto the grass without breaking. I saw a black Labrador dog gulping down the sandwiches which had fallen from my plate. As I looked around I could now see that other people were also laughing whilst watching us laughing and within a few minutes everyone, but Christine, were laughing their heads off at our antics – it was hilarious.

Luckily, we were rescued by the vicar and his wife who were also laughing, and they took away our cups, saucers and plates which gave us a chance to sneak out of the garden for two reasons, one to have a fag and two to calm ourselves down. How embarrassing.

After about fifteen minutes we went back to the vicarage garden to face the music. Much to our relief the vicar told us that it was the best thing that had happened, and it had helped to break the ice with people who didn't know each other. He took us into the vicarage where his wife had made us a ham and cheese sandwich and a proper mug of tea apiece. We were more than grateful and at the same time the vicar's wife was saying that we looked so funny with our little fingers up in the air like you see on television. She also said that she was laughing at our predicament before we were.

The vicar introduced me to Keith, the fireman from Darnall, who whispered to me that he hadn't been bothered about coming today but was glad that he had because he'd had such a good laugh. I was intrigued as to why the church was called after St Lawrence, someone I'd never heard of, so after asking the vicar I was amazed by his answer.

Apparently, St Lawrence was born in Spain in the 2nd century AD. From there he went to Rome and was put in charge of the treasures belonging to the church – wow. Somewhere down the line he was ordered to pass all the treasure onto someone else in Rome other than the church. Instead he distributed it all among the poor, the blind, disabled and anyone who was suffering, which is where he thought it ought to be. For this he was tortured and strapped to a gridiron over hot coals and was slowly roasted alive. Part way through his long and painful roasting he shouted, 'I'm now done on this side, turn me over.' For that comment he later became the patron saint of comedians, the poor, the blind, miners and fire fighters. What a brave man he must have been, and he must have died in agony. No wonder they made the poor bloke a saint.

It was good to mingle with the small crowd, especially the kids and young people. Just as we were about to leave I noticed Keith talking to a chap with the black Labrador that had nicked my sarnies earlier, so I went to speak to them. I love dogs, especially labs, they are so friendly.

As I approached them the man, who was about 45, looked worried and obviously thought he was in bother. He was smartly dressed, and I think he had something to do with the local library. As I bent down to fuss the dog, he apologised about the sandwiches that the dog had eaten, but it took the poor man ages to get his words out. He had, by far, the worst stutter that I have ever heard. On every word his head kept bobbing up and down, with his chin wobbling as he desperately tried to get the words out of his mouth.

'What a cracking dog you have there mate,' I said, 'his coat's lovely and shiny, you obviously think a lot about him.'

'Nnnot rrreally, he's jjjust lllost mmme mmmy wwwife to bbbe. Ssso I'm nnnot happy wwwith him.'

Seeing how difficult it was for him to get his words out, to be honest, was quite upsetting, but realizing he would be used to it all, I asked him why.

'Mmmy ffffiance and I wwwere having a pppicnic in the gggarden and I wwwas ssso happy. The dddog wwwas on his bbbback and my ffffiance wwwas tickling his tummy, and I happened ttto sssay, dddarling wwwhen wwwe are mmmarried you wwwill bbbe able to dddo that to mmme.'

And the poor man then paused before he continued.

'Bbbut bbby the tttime I'd gggot the wwwords out the dddog wwwas licking his balls! That's wwwhy she lllleft mmme.'

I could see that he was very upset.

Both Keith and I looked at each other in amazement at what the poor man had said. Why is it that in situations like this when you're not supposed to laugh you see the funny side of it and it has to come out? How I held onto my laughter for the second time that afternoon, as I ran behind a nearby tree, I don't know, but somehow, I did, and I was inwardly in hysterics at the thought of what he'd just said. I know it wasn't funny to him, and I wasn't laughing at him, but even though I felt guilty I just couldn't help it, and when Keith joined me behind the tree we were just about hysterical. I've never forgotten that afternoon, it was so much fun.

The following day I couldn't wait to tell the lads the story of the dog licking its balls and just like me they thought it was hilarious and we all laughed. I didn't have time to laugh for long as I'd checked the crime reports for anything untoward that might have happened on my area over the weekend.

A burglar alarm had gone off at just after 3am at an electrical shop on Staniforth Road and when the patrol car and night-shift bobby got there they found that there had indeed been a break-in. An alarm going off in those days was investigated immediately as they were few and far between. The owner of the shop was sent for and on his arrival, it was established that only four or five portable radios had been stolen. The thief must have been in and out of there like a shot before the police arrived. After having dealt with that he checked other properties and found that there'd been another break-in on Darnall Terminus, where a newsagent's had been broken into with a loss of cigarettes and tobacco.

I wasn't best pleased as this would be the second time in three weeks that it had happened, although in different premises. This guy needed catching.

Checking the crime reports told me that the rear doors of the properties had been forced open with the use of a crowbar, just the same as the previous ones. So that was at least four break-ins by, what appeared to be, the same person. I later checked with the lad who'd been on nights to ascertain at what time he'd discovered the burglaries. He'd checked both properties prior to 2.30am after which time he'd gone into the little sub-station on Senior Road for his snap. At that time all the premises on his beat were secure.

The Scenes of Crime Department had been out to examine the properties concerned and the crowbar marks where forced entry had been made were all the same size. So, the following weekend, armed with that information, I made sure that I was working the night shift just in case – to catch a burglar you had to think like one. So, come on, let's see if we can catch him, okay? Don't forget your torch.

Burglars tend to be creatures of habit and having been successful on previous jobs it was highly likely that they would go for similar premises in the future. That is if they were local and not just passing through the area. The only premises to have been broken into that had an alarm was the electrical shop but none of the others had one. Friday night – absolutely nothing. The only thing that I'd seen was the night-shift bobby doing his job, shaking hands with all the handles on both the front and back doors, both before and after his meal. I was seriously pissed off, as I'm sure you would have been. A whole shift wasted.

Saturday night was busy with revellers for the first couple of hours and then it went quiet, and I started to think. What if the burglar himself was actually keeping an eye on the policeman on his nightly routine? It wouldn't be the first time that a burglar had waited for the beat bobby to check his properties and when the bobby went on his way, Burglar Bill aka 'Mr Crowbar' would be able to get on with his own nightly work. For that reason and as I had done on previous occasions over the years, I would often, quickly retrace my steps to make sure that there was nobody about.

At about 3am I watched from an alleyway at the side of Wigfall's electrical shop as the night-shift policeman entered into the little police sub-station and switch the light on. He was obviously going for his snap, which we always did at various times of each shift but especially on nights, just in case we were being watched. I was gagging for a pot of tea and could have easily joined him, but I decided to stay where I was. A minute later and much to my amazement, I saw a dark figure dart out of the shadows and quietly tiptoe away from near the sub-station. I could also see that he was carrying a holdall, a bit like the ones that plumbers use. Have we got our man – maybe? As I got to the corner near Darnall Working Men's Club, there was no one to be seen and I was silently cursing like a good un. Where the hell was he? Where had he gone? No matter where I searched he wasn't to be seen again, and by 5am I'd had enough and went home disappointed. The only thing that I was pleased about was the fact that I'd, more than likely, worked out that he'd been waiting for the policeman to go into the sub-station before he made his move, but where had he gone? I'd no idea.

Later the following day when I'd had some kip, I rang the nick only to find out that there had been an attempted burglary at the White Rose pub on Handsworth Road, about three quarters of a mile from where I'd seen the guy with the holdall the night before. The alarm had gone off and when the police arrived they could see marks on the door frame which matched the ones found at the other burglaries that Mr Crowbar had kindly left.

I was going to put myself on night-shift for the whole of the coming week, but then, what was the point. The jobs that he'd done were always on a Friday or Saturday night so, once more on the following Friday night I was on night-shift. Come to Mr Johnson, I thought, I've had enough of you, let me feel your collar.

When the night-shift man came on duty, on Friday night, I explained to him what was what and asked him what time his meal time was and on this particular night it was to be 2.30am. This guy was like Will o' the wisp and it was like trying to find a needle in a haystack, so I took a gamble. I was in my own car and parked it in the alleyway between the Wellington pub and Frank's hairdresser's. From there I could see most of the Terminus where nearly all the shops were situated, and I reasoned that there was a 90 per cent chance of him coming my way – if he came at all, that is. I was glad that I'd brought a flask of tea along with my snap box containing one of my favourites – cold fish and tomato sauce sandwiches. A chunk of home made chocolate cake plus two bananas to follow and after a pot of flask tea and a fag I was ready for action. I wound the car window down to listen for any activity, but it was so quiet you could have heard a mouse fart.

At about 2.10am I could see PC Ken Fox, an old timer, checking the properties on Darnall Terminus, and just before 2.30am he crossed Greenland Road, then into Senior Road. From where I was I couldn't see the sub-station, which didn't really matter. If my theory was right about Mr Crowbar, we should see him in the next few minutes or so – fingers crossed. After pulling a thick pair of heavy woollen socks over my boots to deaden any sound, I sat there like a coiled spring, waiting.

One minute went to two and then three. Suddenly I saw him as he furtively passed almost in front of my car and he then crossed the road towards Child's Chemist's. Technically I should have had three or four other officers placed in strategic positions ready to assist but he was on my patch and I wanted him. As I silently crossed to the chemist I peered around the corner and could see him walking fairly quickly past Lomas's fish and chip shop. He looked to be of average build and was carrying a holdall just like the man I'd seen near the sub-station a week ago. It was Mr Crowbar alright. I managed to follow him without being seen as he passed Ida and Frank Curley's bakehouse at the bottom of Fisher Lane, and then the Conservative Club. As he went around the corner but still on Main Road, I was surprised because there were no shops on that stretch of road. Peeping around the corner I got another surprise – he was nowhere in sight!

At this point you'll have to use your imagination as to what words I was muttering under my breath. I was furious with myself – I'd lost him. Where the hell was he? The only business premises on this bit of road was the Meadow Inn and close to that was the Industry Inn. As I slowly walked towards the pubs, I thought I heard the noise of metal on metal from across the road where the Lyric Cinema was, and I froze. Thirty seconds later I could hear, what to me, was the beautiful sound of splintering wood from up the alleyway leading to the rear of the cinema and I knew that I'd found him. I'd checked these premises regularly and knew that the only way out was to come back down the alleyway, at the corner of which I was now waiting. For my money it was better to allow him to do the job and catch him with his booty rather than grab him now for attempted burglary, so again I waited like a coiled spring.

A few minutes later, he came back down the passageway carrying the bag and I grabbed his left arm, shoved it up his back and grabbed hold of his collar at the back of his neck. At the same time there was a whooshing noise and my helmet was knocked off my head having been hit by the crowbar, which I now knew was in his right hand. He could have bloody killed me. I've never believed in gratuitous violence but when facing a crowbar, I'd no option. Truncheon – no. Fists – yes so I scrambled up from the floor. I managed to hit him full in the face with my left hand. The crowbar fell to the floor, followed by Mr Crowbar who was on his knees, and almost unconscious. I handcuffed him, checked the bag which was full of cigarettes and then dragged him to the little sub-station about a hundred yards away, where he admitted to that and the other burglaries. His face was a mess with a busted nose and both of his eyes were swelling up but, having hit me once with the crowbar, there was no doubt in my mind that he would have tried again if I'd not retaliated with a necessary punch. Wearing a helmet, which was made of cork, was heavy and cumbersome most of the time but that night it saved my life. The helmet was ruined and a new one had to be requisitioned.

Apparently, he lived near the Bradley Well public house near to the sub-station. He worked away during the week on building sites and only came home at weekends.

Later at court he pleaded guilty to all the burglaries and to assaulting yours truly and was sent 'on holiday', to prison, for three to four months, which kept him out of our hair for a while.

CHAPTER 19

'Hans', Knees and Whoops-a-daisy!

As any member of the emergency services will tell you, you never know from one minute to the next what you are likely to come across and that is one of the reasons why life can be very interesting and also at times thought provoking. I have a huge amount of respect for paramedics, ambulance men and women and doctors and nurses in hospitals. That same amount of respect I have for people in the fire brigade, who are often in extremely difficult and dangerous situations. It also applies to the people in the police force and every policeman and woman in the country will, at some time or other, be faced with serious and dangerous situations and all will have had similar experiences to my own. I also admire the road traffic police and especially those on the motorways who, like the fire brigade and ambulance service, are always at the sharp end of the stick when dealing with horrendous accidents.

All the emergency services have one thing in common – they care about YOU and can only do what they think is right at the time without the benefit of hindsight.

After kissing Christine and the kids cheerio I set off to drive to work on the 8am to 4pm shift. It was a grand morning; the birds were singing, and the sun was shining. I hadn't got a care in the world and was looking forward to meeting my good mate Derek Gennard for a pint after work. Turning left at junction 35 of the M1, I joined the south-bound slipway leading onto the motorway itself. From there I could see clouds of smoke hanging over Attercliffe about three miles in front of me, and I chuckled to myself. What birds you did see down there never sang as there was too much pollution and they sounded as if they were smoking forty fags a day, poor things.

Just at the point in the road where I was going to leave the slip road and join the main motorway, my day took a serious turn for the worse.

As I was looking to my right I heard a loud bang and at the same time saw a blue car spinning uncontrollably towards me. Slamming hard on the brakes just saved me from being hit broadside on and the blue car passed maybe two or three inches in front of me and careered through a fence and into a field. At that point I jumped out of my car and, with my heart racing, I grabbed my helmet, just at the same time as I heard another loud bang to my right.

In the near-side lane, I could see a large lorry that was stationary and ran towards it. As I ran alongside it on the hard shoulder I could see a car underneath the back of the lorry having been shunted there by another lorry. From what I could see inside the car, the man was dead. All this had taken seconds. What do you do first? Where do you begin? Other lives are obviously at stake, including my own. Traffic back in those days wasn't as great as it is today but, nevertheless, it was rush hour and I could see three lanes of traffic coming towards me. Without thinking I did one of the most stupid things in my life and ran across the three lanes to the centre of the motorway where I could see and be seen by the oncoming traffic and started to wave my arms about in the air in an attempt to slow them down.

Luckily for us all, and with brakes squealing, the cars and lorries managed to stop in time, in all three lanes. People on the other carriageway, driving in the opposite direction, were rubber necking, obviously having seen what had happened in the south-bound lane. To their credit as they drove slower they were flashing their lights to cars travelling south warning them to slow down. Between them and my own actions it helped to avoid a pile-up. From there I ran across the carriageway again towards the slip road. The poor man in the car was, as near as damn it, decapitated.

As I'd been on my way to work I didn't have a radio with me, but I had to somehow clear the standing traffic on the slip road to allow access for any emergency vehicles and was just hoping that someone, somewhere had rung from an emergency phone at the side of the motorway. Something which, I for one, couldn't see. When you're on your own in a situation like that, when seconds can count, time seems to stand still. People were out of their cars now, both on the motorway itself and the slip road. I was happy that the immediate danger had been averted so I went to check on the occupants of the blue car in the field.

It was an elderly couple who'd both got cuts to their faces, and both were suffering back and neck problems, they were lucky to be alive. I tried to reassure them and calm them down, telling them that the ambulance was on its way and then I went back to the slip road to make sure that the ambulance could get to the scene of the accident. I also knew that the fire brigade would also have to attend with cutting gear to free the poor dead man from his car. From the accident happening to now would, at best, have taken about six or seven minutes.

After making sure the slip road was clear, I went back to the old couple, who were both conscious, and waited with them until the ambulance arrived. I was dying for a fag but the adrenaline had kicked in and I was shaking so much that I wouldn't have held it never mind light it.

Someone had obviously rang 999 and a minute later two ambulances, two motorway patrol cars and a fire engine arrived at the scene. I'd done all I could and after calming myself down I departed having given my details to one of the road traffic officers, whose job it was to deal with the incident.

Arriving at Darnall sub-station I rang the office to tell them why I was late, and then first things first – I was gagging for a pint pot of tea and a fag – and then another fag. There's nothing easy about dealing with circumstances like that and it had shaken me up a bit. My heart went out to the family of the dead man and also to the old couple who, although alive, would obviously suffer problems for the rest of their lives.

Twenty minutes after arriving for work I was back out in the lovely sunshine and looking forward to the rest of the day. I spoke to Jim outside his café on Greenland Road and then Fred and Joan Lee at the Wellington pub who were just opening up for their dinnertime trade, and then as I crossed Staniforth Road walking towards me was my bank manager, Mr Fletcher – if I'd seen him earlier I'd have got out of his way knowing that I was overdrawn.

'Good morning Mr Johnson are you keeping well?'

'Yes, thank you Mr Fletcher and I hope you are too.'

Just as we passed each other he quietly said, 'I hope it's pay day soon Mr Johnson.'

'Yes, OK Mr Fletcher, I think it is.' I chuckled to myself knowing that he was a bit more relaxed this morning but if I'd have seen him in the bank he'd have said, 'Isn't it time you banked with us for a change, Mr Johnson, instead of us banking with you?'

Just then I noticed in front of me a small commotion about thirty yards further down the road. Aye, aye what's going off here I thought. As I got nearer I could see people bending forward and looking at something on the floor, but I couldn't see what it was. As I gently moved the crowd to one side I could see a poor bloke of about 40, dressed in overalls and lying on his front. What I could see of his face was as white as a sheet which wasn't surprising as I could see a pool of blood oozing out from his head. What a bloody mess, I thought. At the side of his head was a house brick and one of the onlookers told me that he'd been walking behind the chap when he heard a funny noise like something sliding down slates. In the next instance he saw the house brick fall and land fairly and squarely on top of the poor chap's head.

'Has anyone sent for an ambulance?' I asked quickly. Nobody seemed to know so I radioed for one immediately.

For all intents and purposes, the man looked dead and the ambulance couldn't come soon enough for me. The pool of blood was getting larger and was coming from a nasty gash at the side of his head and I could see then that part of his skull had been broken. The ambulance must have been fairly close by because it was there within two minutes of my call. According to the ambulance lads he was still alive and they stretchered him into the ambulance and went off with sirens blaring.

Looking up at the high roof from the other side of the road all the brick chimneys appeared to be intact. I contacted the Cleansing Department asking them to come and clean up the blood from the pavement before anyone slipped on it. Back across the road I enquired at several premises as to where the house brick may have come from. No one was working on the roofs and no one knew anything about it, how weird.

When I got back to the sub-station I wrote out an incident report whilst eating my snap. After I'd polished off my pot of tea I rang the hospital for an update of the man. Amazingly he was still alive, and I was told that he should pull through. Papers found in his clothing had allowed the hospital authorities to inform his relatives of his whereabouts.

As I lit a fag I started to ponder over the day's events. I thought about the dead man who had set off to work, just like I had done but he, unfortunately, never got there, poor chap. I thought about the old couple, perhaps going out for the day. They were unlucky to have been injured, but they were lucky to still to be alive. The poor man who was hit on the head with a brick could have easily been killed, but because of expert care, he was lucky to still be with us.

The fire brigade had the nasty job of cutting out the dead body from the car and the ambulance lads had carefully and gently took care of the old couple. The policemen had to deal with the dead driver and then inform his nearest and dearest, a job that we all hated doing. I was also lucky that day. If I'd arrived at the motorway junction two seconds earlier, I could have also been killed, but fortunately I wasn't and managed to avert further serious accidents from happening.

Seeing and dealing with horrible sights and situations can teach us a lesson as anybody in the emergency services will tell you. We all have to live with our aches and pains, life's ups and downs, loneliness or despair. We get on with the life that we have been given, and in the time that we've got left we should all try to live it to the full.

At 4pm I signed off duty and with the aforementioned thoughts in my head I was glad to be going home. I gave Christine and the kids a big love and kiss just as I had done when I left for work that morning, but this time it was a kiss and a love of appreciation that we were all safely together.

After a day like that I can assure you that I was ready for a pint which was handy in view of the fact that I was going to meet my mate Derek Gennard and I knew that somewhere along the line we'd end up with a laugh.

Derek had just started up in business and he'd asked if he could bring someone with him to visit and have supper with us. He was a single bloke and he wanted this person to meet up with a normal English family and he needed to make a good impression. His friend, Hans, was Swedish and Derek was keen to do some business with him in Sweden. Of course, Christine had said yes and now she was busy tidying up and hoovering, getting ready for our visitors. It was a very, very important meeting for Derek and for that reason he wanted to pay for the meal, no matter what the cost. He just wanted it all to work out right.

All of us loved Chinese food so we placed an order with Mr and Mrs Tsang our neighbours at the Chinese takeaway. At that time, we had a dining kitchen, so we set the white, formica-topped, kitchen table out ready. It was an extending table, but we didn't think it necessary to have the middle extension bit in it, so we took it out. We were all set and looking forward to the visit.

I was ready for a few pints after a long day breathing in the smokey Attercliffe air so when Derek and Hans arrived, I took them into the Mason's Arms. The usual old codgers were in the tap room playing crib, including my mates Wilf, Harry and Les who were all in their 70s. More or less in unison they all shouted, 'Where's tha been, we've not seen thi for a week?' I explained to them that I'd been busy and then looked across at Les who looked as though he'd been in a fight. He'd got a plaster over the top of his nose and half a shiner on one eye. He looked in a sorry state.

'What's happened to you Les?'

'Daughter and family are staying, and I've had to lend them mi big potty for under their bed.' Everybody in the room laughed (except poor old Hans who hadn't understood a word).

Les was a great character and we all knew his almost daily routine. He'd have a few pints at dinner time, home to bed and a potty under the bed so as not to disturb anybody when he got up for a wee.

'What's that got to do with your shiner Les?'

'I had to lend t'family mi big potty from under t'bed which I use during t'night. So, I ended up using grandkids little plastic potty with a straight handle on it.'

What is he on about? I thought, then he unhappily continued, 'I went up to bed after dinner for a nap and when I got up I had a piss in t'potty. And when I put mi trousers on I started to pull mi braces up over mi shoulders but they hooked on t'handle o t'bloody potty. Potty hit me on t'back o t'head, piss and all, and it pitched me forward and a banged mi head on't door. I was glad when they went bloody hom.'

Everybody was in hysterics except poor Hans, who had obviously never heard broad Yorkshire spoken before and he had no idea what I was talking about never mind Les.

A couple of pints later with Hans shaking his head and not knowing what, was what, we went back home to a 'normal' English household.

Back at home and now all hungry after a few pints, everything was ready, and with great ceremony Christine brought in the meal from the takeaway and set it out on the table. Plates and cutlery had been set out and all four of us sat down to eat. We helped ourselves to the various dishes which looked and smelled delicious. Our plates were filled, and we were all ready to start.

As soon as Hans put pressure on his plate with his knife and fork the table, which had a split in the middle to accommodate the extension leaf, suddenly tipped up and in what seemed like slow motion, the whole meal slid off the table and ended up on the poor man's knee. Christine nearly passed out, Derek and I looked at each other in disbelief and poor Hans jumped up in the air. He was in a right mess and was dancing up and down because of the hot sweet and sour sauce that was now stuck to his shirt and trousers, burning his legs and unmentionables! Sweet and sour chicken balls took on a different meaning that night. Why is it in situations like this, that we laugh when we aren't supposed to. I was inwardly in hysterics. The sight of Christine with a wet towel trying to sponge poor Hans' burning balls down creased me up big style. Our two dogs were skidding around his ankles trying to recover the free food that had landed on the floor and poor Derek just stood there with his mouth open as he looked on in amazement.

Which idiot had forgotten to fasten the two leaves of the table together when he took out the extension? I'll give you one guess – I admitted to it and apologized – and I felt a right twerp. I didn't know whether to stutter, laugh or stammer as I tried to explain to Hans that it was a quaint English custom! Poor old Christine was in a state of shock, but luckily Hans was a good guy with a sense of humour and saw the funny side of it.

Thankfully, Derek got the business in spite of the antics of a far from 'normal' English family. The poor man's suit was ruined and as they left our house the dogs were following him. Christine, Derek and Hans survived the shock and even today, forty years after the event, we still laugh about that 'Hans', knees and whoops-a-daisy night.

Note: I would like to dedicate this chapter to all the emergency services in the land, none of us are perfect and can only help the community that we serve without the benefit of hindsight.

CHAPTER 20

Dead Beat?

My mum Esther was a prolific letter writer and especially so to our relatives in Canada. From an early age we got occasional Canadian relatives coming to stay with us for a couple of weeks. They were, in the main, older people who had emigrated to Canada many years ago, as children with their parents, who were looking for work. Now retired and having made a few quid they could afford to come and visit us. Mum and dad made them all welcome and my dad, Fred, always wanted to reciprocate their visits and take mum to Canada.

Because of working down the pit and having twice been almost buried alive because of roof collapses, dad suffered bad health. In 1976, he had to have a minor hip operation during which he unexpectedly and sadly passed away, aged 63 – four hours before our seventh wedding anniversary. We were distraught. Dad was a very popular and funny, family man and because Darfield churchyard was so badly overgrown at that time I was contacted by his big pal from the pit, Jack Croft.

'Neither Fred or thi mam, Esther, are going to get darn t'bottom o' that churchyard, wi' state it's in lad – leave it up to me, Martyn,' Jack said; and off he went.

We all got a shock on the day of dad's funeral as we got to the church. There were so many people there and Jack and all the miners had lined the route on both sides of the pathway leading to the bottom of the, now cleared churchyard. What a brilliant job the miners did for us that day and some of them made sure that it never got overgrown again, by later forming The Friends of Darfield Churchyard Group.

A few months later, when mum had come round a bit, I thought it was the right time to keep the promise that I'd made to dad. Along with my young sister, Liz, we took mum to Canada to see her long-lost relatives at a family reunion that had been organized for our visit. None of us had flown before and we thoroughly enjoyed the flight to Toronto. At the family gathering we were amazed to see so many relatives, some of whom had flown in from different parts of Canada to be there to meet mum. Mum loved it and, because she was the first relative to visit Canada, she was treated like the Queen. Liz and I were spellbound by it all, as we were met by so many people with different surnames, such as Jackson, Fenton, Wilshire, Leggit and Watson, and they were all somehow related to us.

The gathering was organized by Bud and Muriel Leggit who lived in a gorgeous house on what they called a dirt road. The house number was 25552, I couldn't believe it, they must live on the longest road in the world.

Bud was a World War Two veteran and had received a bravery medal for his actions in battle. He, along with his daughter Mary, were also a well-known Country and Western singing duo. Mary's husband Terry amazed me by saying that he was an avid follower of Sheffield Wednesday Football Club and proudly pointed to his car registration number SWF 1. Mary and Terry were great and during the rest of our two-week trip they and other relatives very kindly took us everywhere.

We stood in total awe at the power and sight of the huge Niagara Falls and as we walked to the Skylon Tower, I was amazed to see, running about on the grass black squirrels and blue jays flying in and out of the trees. Surely nothing could beat that. The Skylon Tower was amazing and even though I get dizzy wearing two pairs of socks, we went to the top. The views were amazing, but I was glad when we got down.

On another day we went to the beautiful city of Toronto where the Canadian National Tower had recently been built, the top of which, at 1800 feet, I'm sure touched the sky, and at that time it was the tallest building in the world! I didn't want to know about going up in it but as Liz quite rightly said, we'll never get the chance again, so in we went. It was terrifying and to make matters worse the doors of the outside lift were made of glass. Someone pressed a button and up we went like a space rocket, and as we got out at the top, after my stomach had caught up with me, it was breathtaking and on odd occasions we were looking down on a small aeroplane that was flying below us – amazing. We were very lucky one day when another relative, Kath Weatherill, took us to the Canadian National Exhibition Centre, her husband Lloyd was one of the officials there, which meant that we had free access. It was nothing short of incredible, there was so much to see and do and it could only be described as being like Disney World is today.

One of the things that caught my attention whilst I was there was a massive American police patrol car which was being shown, for some reason, at the exhibition. A policeman was standing with the car and I couldn't wait to speak to him. I'd brought along with me one or two badges in case I met another policeman. I went to talk to him and gave him a couple of badges and he in turn passed me one of his. He was only small for a policeman and also rather round, which surprised me.

As we chatted he asked me, in an American drawl, if it was true that we only carried a small piece of wood (truncheon) to defend ourselves with, to which I replied that, yes that was correct. This he found hard to believe, which didn't surprise me as I could see that he was carrying a gun in a holster. Rather naively, I asked him if he'd ever had to use the gun he was carrying, and he looked at me in amazement as he said that at times he could use it daily. At the same time, he opened the boot of the black and white patrol car which shook me rigid as it was full of every type of automatic weapons that you could imagine, and my mouth must have dropped open.

Again naively, I asked him if he had ever killed anybody with a gun. I'll never forget his reply. He said, 'Sir, I must shoot someone dead every few weeks.' He wasn't showing off or gloating but just stating facts and I could see that he meant it. What an eye opener.

Back home, our Police Federation had, on one or two occasions, asked us if we, ourselves, would like to carry guns for protection but none of us did. We were alright as we were. What's gone wrong between then and now? Armed police are all over the place, how times have changed.

The visit cheered mum up. Elizabeth, mum and I had really enjoyed seeing our Canadian relatives and a bit of Canada. But the main thing for me was that I'd kept my promise to dad and the whole experience for us all was wonderful. I was really glad that we'd done it all, but I was also glad when my feet were firmly back on English soil.

When I got home I looked at my wooden truncheon and realized that I would much rather have that to protect me than having shot someone on my conscience.

It was good to get back home, I'd really missed Christine and the kids. Leaving them behind and going on my own had been a hard decision to make, but several years later I made amends and took Christine, Richard, Sally, Paul and Amanda to Canada and they all loved it. Mum's batteries were recharged, and the trip had helped to take her mind of losing dad.

The downside to me was that by the time we got back from Manchester airport I felt as rough as a bear's bum. I'd heard people talk about 'jet-lag', whatever that was, and because I'd never flown before I assumed that that was what I was suffering from. I wasn't one for doctors and to go off sick I would have to have been at death's door. Whatever I'd got I couldn't shake it off, but even though my head felt like a bucket I arrived for work at Darnall sub-station at 7am on Sunday morning.

Harold Singleton was the sergeant on duty and working one of the beats at Darnall was young Graham Glover (the fairly new lad who'd dealt with the 'soggy foot' man in the canal). Sergeant Singleton took one look at me and said that I looked shocking and didn't ought to be at work, but although Graham drove his own car he hadn't been on the job long enough to have taken his police driving exam. The other bloke, Ken Fox, who should have been on duty and could drive the police car, had phoned in sick himself, so it left me being the only driver. That was the last thing I'd wanted. I was the 'area' bobby not the 'regular shift' bobby.

Harold wasn't best pleased, one probationer policeman, one off sick and myself who should have been off sick.

'Martyn, I'm sorry about this, I know you're rough but help me out and have this new lad with you the whole shift. Sunday's are normally quiet, go and park up somewhere and have a kip.'

Harold was a good man, so Graham and I, along with a packet of headache tablets, drove up to High Hazels Park, where I got my head down and nodded off. We were lucky that morning as nothing untoward happened. At about 11am we went back to the little nick so that Graham could have his snap. A couple of times during the morning I'd been sick and so I couldn't face any food and all I could think of was 3pm and home to bed. After snap time I parked the police car up on the old Darnall dog track where it was quiet, and prayed for nothing to happen.

Twelve noon, 1pm, 2pm nothing – thank goodness for that and 3 o'clock couldn't come soon enough for me. I was getting worse not better. If this is bloody jet-lag, I'll not be flying again! At about 2.15pm the car radio went: 'Attend such and such an address on Richmond Park Road, neighbours reporting that another neighbour hasn't been seen and after knocking on her door they can't get any response and they're worried.'

Five minutes later we were there at a small block of flats where we could see a few of the locals standing about waiting for our arrival and they all had a concerned and worried look on their faces. One of the neighbours, who was a retired nurse, had had the foresight to send for the doctor who lived just around the corner so that, if she was ill, he could attend to her quickly.

The three of us, the doctor, Graham and myself were shown which flat the lady lived in by one of the neighbours and so I knocked on the door but there was no response whatsoever; and I thought that the neighbours were right in thinking the worst. If she was ill she needed urgent attention. No one had a key to the flat which left us with no option but to break down the door. Graham was a big strong lad and the door went the first time and we were inside.

It was all new to Graham and he was obviously concerned about what we would find. She wasn't in the small sitting room or the tiny kitchen, so here we go, last room bedroom and there she was. I could see straight away that she was dead and after the doctor checked for a pulse it proved to be correct and he certified the death. On her bedside table was an empty box of tablets, at the side of which was a beautifully hand-written note, which read at the start: 'I am old and tired of living like this, I have no relatives, so I have decided to take my own life and am quite happy to do so.' The concluding sentence was: 'I apologize to whoever finds me dead'. How sad for a lady to feel like that and how brave to do what she did.

After the doctor went I explained to Graham that because he had certified 'death' – but not the cause, even though it was fairly obvious – the lady would have to go to the city mortuary for a post-mortem to take place. It was a straightforward job to us and I rang the nick from the old lady's landline at 3.10pm and spoke to Inspector Radford. I explained the situation and the fact that I was ill and should have been off duty ten minutes ago. It appeared to be a straight forward suicide so could he ring the mortuary and ask them to attend to remove the body and, if possible, get someone to take over from me and Graham.

Ten minutes later he rang me back, 'Sorry about this Martyn, we're all busy so I can't replace you, and it being Sunday afternoon, the mortuary people have only got a skeleton staff! Unfortunately it's going to be three to four hours before they can get to you.' I couldn't believe it, what the hell was I going to do for three to four hours, I was getting worse by the minute and wasn't happy at all. My head was pounding. I explained to Graham we were 'stuck lad'. Graham switched on the pink-screen television in the small sitting room and sat down in a chair to watch it for a couple of hours to pass the time on. What a palaver, I thought.

I'd just been sick again in the toilet and was feeling absolutely crap. Going into the bedroom, I looked at the old lady laid on the bed and called Graham.

'What's up?'

'I'm desperate – right, I want you to get your hands under the bedclothes and hold the lady's feet while I hold her head, okay?'

'Why, what are you doing?'

'We'll just move her to the edge of the bed.'

As we did so he looked at me in amazement as I removed my police tunic and boots and, facing away from her, I laid down next to her but on top of the bed covers. A few seconds later I was 'dead' to the world!

According to Graham, the mortuary van arrived, as near as damn it, about four hours later. The mortuary attendant looked at us both on the bed and asked Graham which one was the corpse, as I looked as bad as the old lady did.

The deceased lady was removed and taken to the mortuary where it was later confirmed that she had committed suicide by taking an overdose of tablets.

Graham never let me live it down. From where he was sitting he could see us both laid on the bed in the nearby bedroom. The lady was at rest and so was I, apart from snoring, farting and belching for about four hours.

From never before being off work sick for more than a few days, I ended up being off for three weeks whilst on antibiotics.

It was assumed that I'd picked up a virus or something in Canada, but whatever it was it certainly knocked me for a six. Looking back on that day now I can laugh about it, but it certainly wasn't funny to me at the time.

Just before getting back to work, Graham phoned to tell me that he had arranged for us both to go clay-pigeon shooting with some farmers and his mates somewhere on Whitely Lane in Ecclesfield one Sunday morning. Both he and I did a bit of rough shooting on the Wentworth estate near where I lived.

When farmers sowed their seeds in the surrounding fields near to where hundreds of wood pigeons roosted it was a big problem. Flocks of the pigeons could strip a field of its crops within hours. The estate used to call upon people like Graham and myself – along with the gamekeepers – to try and alleviate the situation. Graham, especially, loved it as did the farmers who appreciated the help. For this reason, they'd organized a clay shoot for us all to get in some practice. I wasn't bothered about going but having been invited I thought I'd better attend, but I wished that I'd stayed in bed instead.

I'd never been clay shooting before and didn't realize that you were booked in for a certain time for your turn to shoot. I decided to take the kids along with me and, as it was a cold day, we were all togged up in warm clothes. I was wearing my Barbour coat.

When we arrived at the venue I could see people that I knew including Graham, Frank Peat (the milkman) along with his sons, 'Malc the milk', Nigel and Chris, along with Steven Rhodes from a nearby farm. Apparently, I was late, and Graham was jumping up and down and cursing. He passed me his 'over and under' shotgun, something that I'd never used before, as I normally used a 'side by side' shotgun. There were some rough blokes there and I could hear the occasional snide remarks about 'bloody coppers', which I tried to ignore.

Graham passed me a load of cartridges which I stuffed into my Barbour pocket. Never having shot at clays before, being late and using Graham's gun instead of my own made me feel self-conscious because everybody was watching me. Somebody shouted, 'PULL' and the two clays went flying into the air in different directions. I lifted the gun and fired at them both and, much to my annoyance, missed, and the crowd was sniggering which unnerved me all the more. If they'd have been pigeons I wouldn't have missed. The next thing someone shouted 'PULL' again and two more went up and I missed again. I could see from Graham's face that I was embarrassing him, and I felt a right twerp as the crowd once more was sniggering away.

I grabbed two more cartridges out of my pocket and was determined that the next two would be mine. The crowd went quiet as this time I shouted, 'PULL' and just before the clays were released Graham shouted, 'WHOA, WHAT ARE YOU DOING?' and 'BREAK YOUR GUN' (which means open it).'

'What do you mean – break my gun? What for?'

'Martyn, just break your gun,' he said quietly as the crowd also went quiet. 'Remove the cartridges,' he then whispered; and as I did so I couldn't believe what I'd stupidly done. Whenever I went shooting I always had, in my Barbour coat pocket, a tube of Polo mints and in my haste I'd put a cartridge in one barrel and a tube of Polos in the other. I went as red as a beetroot. The crowd was in uproar and a rough bloke who was about 6' 6" and stood at the back of the crowd shouted, 'WHAT'S THAT DOZY PILLOCK DOING, IS HE TRYING TO SHOOT 'EM OR RING 'EM?' (racing pigeons always have identity rings on their legs).

Everyone was in uproar with laughing apart from me and Graham. After passing him his gun back, I rounded the kids up and we slinked away. It was one of the most awkward days of my life.

Everybody who was there that day that I knew has never let me forget about it and I was too embarrassed to go clay-pigeon shooting ever again.

Graham didn't speak to me for two weeks after that!

I hope you have enjoyed working the beat with me again, dealing with different situations. Health permitting, you may be able to join me in the next book when I leave the police force and go back into 'Civi Street', where there will be both laughs and clangers.

Thank you for your continued support and I wish you all the very best.

Martyn